CAST
CATCH
RELEASE

CAST CATCH RELEASE

MARINA GIBSON

hodder
press

First published in Great Britain in 2024 by Hodder Press
An imprint of Hodder & Stoughton Limited
An Hachette UK company

I

Copyright © Marina Gibson 2024

The right of Marina Gibson to be identified as the Author of the Work has been
asserted by her in accordance with the Copyright, Designs and Patents Act 1988.

Internal illustrations © Jonathan Gibbs

A CIP catalogue record for this title is available from the British Library

Hardback ISBN 9781529394320
Trade Paperback ISBN 9781529394337
ebook ISBN 9781529394344

Typeset in Bembo MT by Hewer Text UK Ltd, Edinburgh
Printed and bound in Great Britain by Clays Ltd, Elcograf S.p.A.

Hodder & Stoughton policy is to use papers that are natural, renewable
and recyclable products and made from wood grown in sustainable
forests. The logging and manufacturing processes are expected to
conform to the environmental regulations of the country of origin.

Hodder Press
Hodder & Stoughton Limited
Carmelite House
50 Victoria Embankment
London EC4Y 0DZ

www.hodderpress.co.uk

In loving memory of Sedge, Uncle Timothy and Mick May.

Contents

Prologue

The Sécure River, a tributary of the Amazon River.

The trees loomed all around me, as if in silent judgement. Even those perched on nearby clifftops seemed to be watching as I brought back my elbow to make the cast. My eyes were focused downward, on a faint glimmer in the water that told me now was the moment to act.

I had come to Bolivia in search of a rare, almost miraculous fish about which every angler dreams. Known as the river tiger, the golden dorado is the apex predator of the waters that flow through the Amazon rainforest and one of the most powerful game-fish in the world. It shimmers seductively when its head of ethereal, burnished gold emerges from the water, before opening its mouth to reveal the tack-sharp teeth and piston-strong jaw that make it such a ferocious adversary to both hunter and prey. When a golden dorado is on the hook and trying to run, the water does not just ripple; it boils. A foamy froth of fight and flight. Of all the fish I have sought around the world, this was the one I had really been waiting for and for which I had come so far, in so many ways. Early in the trip I had hooked into a few little ones, but now the end of the week was nearing and the true experience, the monster catch, still eluded me. I knew I could not leave the rainforest without it.

'Either the jungle will accept you, or it will spit you out,' our guide had told us on the first day of the trip. For that week I felt as if it had swallowed me whole; so intense were the colours and noises, so vast and foreboding the dense landscape, it was sometimes hard to imagine anything could exist beyond its epic reaches. Macaws screeched overhead and the humid air seemed to hum with swarms of tiny sandflies (I had already been bitten red through the mesh holes in my leggings earlier in the week). While we fished, bright butterflies would land around us in a confetti stream of flying colours, uncoiling their feeding tubes to sip the salt.

This was the Sécure River, a tributary of a tributary of a tributary that flows into the mighty Amazon. For days we had been traversing it via wooden canoe, through narrow stretches where the banks closed in and the canopy enveloped us, to wider ones where the trees retreated to let the water run wide, round boulders that pockmarked its surface, each one a potential hiding place for the dorado. Most of the banks were rocky but some were beachy; the guides told us to shuffle our boots through the sand, warding off any stingrays that may be buried below its surface.

With my fishing partner and guide further up the pool, I felt completely alone in this wilderness, my boots gripping the bank's smooth stones, gazing into water made cloudier than it would normally have been by a recent flood. After my brush with the sandflies, I had started wearing long, thin trousers, which clung to my legs in the sticky heat.

Yet even in such intense immersion, I could not banish the thoughts I had come all this way to escape. While I had come to Bolivia in search of the golden dorado, I was also desperately running away from something. My marriage, less than two years old, already seemed destined to fail.

I had retreated to the jungle to get away and lose myself in the most extreme fishing environment there is. But I couldn't concentrate. The serenity that angling usually provides was now like a radio signal dropping in and out, a burst of self-recriminating static regularly interrupting the calm. Even in this remote setting, thousands of miles from my home in England, the questions had followed me. How had it come to this? Could it really end so soon? What would people say?

When finally, under a broken tree trunk dipping into the water, I saw the hint of gold, part of me knew I should wait. Back home I was accustomed to using simpler knots, but I knew that here I would need to make the teardrop shape of the perfection loop, the knot needed to attach the fly securely enough to withstand the dorado's brutal bite. I could just see Lucas, our guide, but he was too far away to call out to. I knew that this was *my* tiger, the fish I had come here to land, and I didn't dare let the moment pass. Instinct kicked in and my fingers went to work on an improved clinch knot, taking the end of the line, threading the fly and wrapping it five times round itself. Then through the loops, first small then large, wetting the knot in my mouth before pulling both ends tight. It was really a knot for trout or salmon, but it would have to do.

Fly tied, I made a quick cast under the target and stripped the line back with my right hand until I felt the reassuring thud of the fish locking its jaws on to the lure. Not yet the ferocious tug I was expecting – that would come once I had 'set' my hook, securing it in the mouth of the fish to begin the process of reeling it in.

If this were a trout, I would only need to smartly lift the rod tip, a single vertical motion. But in the hard, unforgiving mouth of the golden dorado, something more was needed: a 'strip strike', a hard, lateral tug on the line with my hand to exert maximum pressure and fix the hook firmly in place. I got ready, bracing my feet to take the full weight of the fish's resistance, expecting to feel the satisfaction of the set.

But suddenly I felt only slack. The trees still towered, the butterflies still hovered and the macaws still called, but the fish had gone.

Just as quickly, the hot, humiliating realisation dawned. There had been no failure of casting technique, or in how I had tried to set my hook. The problem was more fundamental, with the knot I had so hastily tied, rushing to seize the opportunity rather than waiting for help to arrive. It had simply snapped under the strain. It was an embarrassing error, at the worst possible moment, like a runner tripping over their own untied shoelaces as they leave the starting blocks. Minutes later Lucas was there, giving the rueful smile of someone who had seen this all before. 'Why didn't you wait for me?'

The snapped fly was more than a catch lost, more than a bucket-list fish slipping from my grasp. It was a wake-up call; I was making bad decisions, my mind as out of control as my life was starting to feel. So often fishing had been my one guarantee against this – a chance to unhook my mind and take respite from the thoughts thrashing around as I stumbled through each day, trying to pretend that everything was normal and I could function perfectly fine.

But now, with my marriage curdling even before reaching its cotton anniversary, let alone something more precious, the one door I had always been able to barricade myself behind no longer held. Months of denial were catching up with me. The strain had become too great.

And even as fishing appeared to fail me, it still pointed the path forward. Until now I had been suspended in a state of fear and doubt, unable to take a step forward or back. Now I had clarity. Even as I felt the frustration flood through me, for the fish I had desperately sought but somehow let slip, for the marriage I had so believed in but had now lost faith in, I knew what I had to do. It could be delayed no longer.

The day after I got home from Bolivia, the decision was made, the knot untied.

It would not be the first time that fishing had helped pull me out of desperation, throwing out a line onto which to cling, and helping me find the answers I could not find anywhere else. Nor would it be the last.

CAST

Chapter 1

The River Spey, Scotland.

'Did your dad get you into fishing?'

It's a question I have been asked more times than I can remember, at fishing lakes and on riverbanks. But it wasn't my dad who first took me fishing, showing me how to attach a fly and cast a line. For me, fishing has always been with my mum; she was my first teacher, my greatest inspiration, and she is still my ideal fishing partner.

She is there in my first memories, by our local trout pond in Gloucestershire, as I swing a shrimp net around, scooping up whatever mixture of wriggling, flying and floating things I could find. Warning me and my older brother Marcus to be quiet, not to scare the fish away by shouting or splashing. Back then there was no technique for me; no knowledge of fishing or thought to the connection between the rod and the loops that the line must form. Just the water, a still surface concealing a universe of mysteries. I loved the water before I even knew what fishing was; before I had ever held a fishing rod in my hand, felt the wet skin of a fish wriggling across my palms, or seen the sheen of its body up close.

In time, my mum showed me how fishing is done and what it means, sharing the love of water and sport that she had nurtured since childhood, catching bullheads and stickleback by hand in the brook that ran by her home in Warwickshire. We had been fishing together since the very beginning; eight months pregnant with me and unable to wade into deep water, she was standing atop a gorge on the Isle of Lewis, the air thick with midges as she cast the line.

'I've never been to the Outer Hebrides,' I once ventured.

'Oh but you have,' she told me.

The water and everything beneath it were at the heart of a childhood spent outdoors whenever possible, usually with my brother – tending to the animals we kept, walking our dogs in the nearby woods, and nagging Mum to take us out to the trout pond. Whatever we did, we competed over. On weekend and school holiday mornings, Marcus and I would race to be first out of our house in Stow-on-the-Wold, dashing through the courtyard and beyond the wooden gate that seemed so massive to my six-year-old self. Buckets of feed in hand, we would enter the chicken run with some trepidation, on watch for the cockerel that sometimes rushed towards us, attacking with its spurs, those singular claws that curve backward from their legs like little rhino horns. The chickens were just one part of an animal collection that sometimes made our home resemble a miniature farmyard. Inside were our dogs, cats, hamsters, tadpoles and stick insects. Next to the front door I would find garden snails on the creepers and bring them inside, one at a time, to build houses for them, admiring the shiny trails they left along the floors and up the walls.

Among the blurry memories of early childhood, certain details retain the sharp edges of discovery: the languid, curving legs and tail of the mayfly that clustered around the trout pond where I first learned to fish, the obsidian bodies of water beetles, and a newt's splayed limbs and mottled skin. I remember thinking that it was a dinosaur in miniature, as if it had walked straight off the page of one of my picture books.

A few years on from these first fragments, memories start to form: I have brought paints with me to the water, collecting pebbles to decorate, choosing those smooth enough to fit snugly in my palm but large enough for my brushes to work on. My parents are fishing further down the river, my mother immaculate in tweed, my father in a familiar blue jumper, despite the Scottish summer air. I love watching them cast: Dad upright, using every inch of his commanding physique to compel the fly across the river's full width; Mum smooth and serene, every movement precise, working with the water and wasting no effort. They fish and I paint, while the river sighs its way past.

A little pile of my stones has built up, drying on the riverbank in the pale sunshine, when I catch sight of it. The glint of the sun on something that is not where it should be: the translucent wing of a dragonfly, lying on the bank. Barely breathing for fear of disturbing it, I move a little closer and squint at the insect's spindly dark legs and its spiky abdomen, patterned black and blue. It remains motionless. After a while I realise that it is not resting but dead; its final flight had landed right by me, without my having noticed. It had been born from the water in front of me, hatched from an egg laid there, and it had returned to the precipice of the river to die.

Holding it gently by the tail, I scoop the dragonfly up in the palm of my hand. Its little body is both delicate and robust; its four wings, once capable of propelling it through the sky at impressive speed, are gossamer thin, tiny dark veins running over them like crazy-paving. I decide I will take it home with me to treasure, along with the rocks I have spent most of my day decorating. At home we will varnish the rocks; some will be used as doorstops and the rest I will store on the windowsill of my bedroom, a reminder of the summer gone and the promise of another one to come.

'What's that?'

So engrossed am I that I don't notice Jamie standing next to me. My family is holidaying with his and in the future he will be a friend. But now he is just a boy, doing as boys do, asking questions and making demands, insisting that they be allowed to join in. I cradle my dragonfly protectively, one palm overlapping the other.

'I've seen you with your stupid rocks.'

'They're not stupid.'

'Stupid.' He picks up one from my pile and throws it far into the water. I watch it disappear, swallowed soundlessly by the current's steady hum.

'Don't.'

'*Stupid.*' Another rock is thrown.

He turns to look at me, his face taunting. In my fury, suddenly my hand is not cradling and protecting. It opens, and we watch as the dragonfly's body drifts back to the ground.

It is as though we both know what is going to happen next.

As he lifts his foot and then stamps down on the lifeless body, my hand closes into a fist and I punch him full in the face. He is screaming and now adult voices are the ones being raised. There are stern words, reluctant apologies, solemn promises that it will never happen again. My crushed dragonfly lies forgotten; some of the rocks will be salvaged, but back home they will always tell a different story from the one I had painted onto them.

The spawning of the Atlantic salmon is both an end and a beginning. For both the mature male and female salmon, it is the culmination of a journey that has taken them from their home rivers out into the perils of the ocean, to feed, grow and ultimately return: one of nature's great tales of there and back again. Often years have passed since the salmon swam in these fresh waters, the same ones that washed them into this world. Now they must address the purpose to which their continent-spanning journey over thousands of miles has brought them.

The female salmon waits until the cool waters of autumn or early winter to lay her eggs. She seeks out a riffle, an area of the river where the water is shallow and flows faster, and the sediment is coarser – gravel rather than silt, a stable basis to build her nest. Here the rapid water flow improves oxygen levels and prevents too many other nests being made in the same area, averting a concentration of hatchlings that would encourage predators and intensify competition for food.

With her tail, the salmon beats and brushes the riverbed, dislodging stones and gravel to create a depression that will serve as her nest, known as a redd. Close at hand is her mate, attracted by the pheromones the female has released, and attentive to any competing male salmon. As soon as the eggs have been laid in the redd, he will immediately move in to fertilise them with milt. She then covers them over with newly displaced gravel, sealing one redd and creating another. Together, the pair will repeat this ritual several more times in close succession until the female has released all her eggs, leaving thousands of these orange-red globes buried across multiple redds, their sticky surfaces helping them adhere to each other and to the gravel river bottom.

During this process, the movements of the fish and the flow of the river will dislodge some of the eggs, propelling them beyond the safety of the redd for ever. These eggs are just the first victims of the precipitous odds that Atlantic salmon face at all stages of their lives. Winter will claim more casualties before the eggs have even had a chance to hatch. Of the thousands of eggs laid by the female salmon during her spawning, just a handful will survive into adulthood to breed themselves.

For the eggs that survive, hatching will begin in early spring, prompted by the rising water temperatures. Within the egg, now a milky pearl, the bright eye of the baby salmon has visibly come to life. Its body is becoming too strong to be contained any longer. It begins to move inside the egg, to wriggle and struggle against its confinement. The shuddering movement of one egg prompts another, and they begin to hatch in a chain reaction.

The hatchlings emerge as alevin, worm-like and translucent. They are strong enough to escape the confines of the egg, but not yet to leave the redd. For another month or two they will exist in a liminal space between birth and life, still living in the nest that protects them, with the remnants of the egg attached to their underside, the colour of golden yolk, providing the nutrients for an infant still unable to feed independently. Only after its contents have been fully absorbed is the alevin ready to leave the redd and begin its life in the river.

'Come on!'

It's summertime, and a breeze idles across the fast-flowing surface of the river. Slicing diagonally across the north-east of the country, the Spey is a waterway twisted through Scotland's history and its great industries. It flows down from the Monadhliath Mountains – the 'grey hills' – its tea-stained waters traversing channels that were first cut into the land by retreating Ice Age glaciers, their meltwater streams carving paths, merging into rivers and forming waterfalls at the junctures where hard rock gives way to soft. The Spey then wends north across the Cairngorms, through glens, fir and birch forests, past distilleries that draw on its waters to produce whisky, and former shipbuilding towns that once relied on it to transport wood, and on through the Morayshire countryside, until it spills into the North Sea at the midpoint between Portknockie and Lossiemouth.

Over its hundred miles, the Spey is witness to a remarkable panoply of wildlife: Eurasian otters that fish its waters as assiduously as any human angler; ospreys that patrol above, plunging to pluck a fish; red deer that can occasionally be seen wading across, antlers bowed to drink.

But the one creature with which the Spey is truly synonymous is the Atlantic salmon. Each year thousands of fish will complete their migration by returning to its waters, a final hundred miles after the many more they have swum to reach the river mouth. After them anglers follow, crowding the river's lower courses, which comprise some of the most famous salmon-fishing beats in the world. For an angler in pursuit of salmon, the Spey is the most hallowed of waters, its banks sacred ground beneath our feet. But in my child's mind it is simply somewhere to fish, by now with a rod and line, as I learn the basics of the craft. I am eight years old; a novice, and an impatient one. I feel sure that time on a fishing trip spent anywhere except on the riverbank is time wasted.

The adults in our party, my parents and godfather among them, do not agree. They are a little distance away, still enjoying the picnic lunch that I have torn through in my eagerness to get back.

I can hear their conversation, rising above the gentle rush of the river and the high-pitched muttering of a sparrowhawk or oystercatcher. I pace up and down, flattening the grass with my wellies, waiting and waiting for lunch to be over so I can begin again. No one seems to have noticed that I have wandered off.

'Come *on*.'

I can feel my frustration bubbling up. 'She's like a bottle of fizz,' a teacher will later say of me, describing the enthusiasm tinged with urgency that I will learn both to appreciate and bemoan – a trait that can spark impulsive decisions, with exactly the sort of outcomes that impulsive decisions can lead to.

No more waiting. I grab a rod from the rack, its line threaded and the fly still tied on. Designed to be gripped with both hands, it is bigger than I can easily handle and lurches a little as I pick it up, but the feel of the cork grip in my palms, one that will become so familiar, is already comfortable. I stomp down to the bank and start casting.

Earlier that day I had learned the technique synonymous with this river – the Spey cast. A ghillie, one of the traditionally Scottish guides who maintains the river and helps visitors to fish it, had taken Marcus and me out on a little boat. We went round and round the pool – a deep, slow-moving section of the river – him showing us the graceful circular sweep that sends the line into a D-shaped loop before you bring it back onto the surface of the water. My mother said we looked like the Owl and the Pussycat, turning circles in the little boat and casting loops with our fishing rods, two small children and one silver-haired, tweed-capped man.

Now I am eager, if not ready, to put this lesson into practice. I have no technique. Although I know what good casting *looks* like, I am still not, by any reasonable definition, fishing; the movements of my shoulders and arms are lumpy where they should be smooth, propelled by brute force rather than rhythm. I yank the line back, dragging it round and up over my shoulder before hurling it forward onto the water. I do this again and again, a bad imitation of the real thing that still feels good because I am doing something, and something is always better than nothing.

I don't know how long I have been doing this before it happens. A jolt of surprise bursts through my stomach as the line tightens; nerve endings start firing. My brain registers that there is weight on the end of the line and I realise that a fish has taken the fly. Not one of the Spey's signature salmon, but another migratory fish that returns to its waters – a sea trout. The thing I have been hoping for has happened, both at long last and before I know what to do. I still feel that little explosion every time I hook into a fish today, even though I am casting deliberately, towards a target I have identified, and there is rarely any element of pure surprise. But that day, the first day, surprise overwhelms me. The fish writhes on the line and the rod twists and shakes in my hands. I am shouting – thrilled and terrified, completely unsure what I am supposed to do next, feeling as if I have won but also afraid I am about to lose.

In time I will learn that the moment the fish takes the fly, biting down on the lure, is when you must let the emotion drain out of you. That fish are landed not in a frenzy of excitement but with patient precision. When a strong fish has decided to run, careering away from its hunter and trying to shake off the hook, it needs to be given enough line, enough room to fight until it is ready to come in. It is a matador's dance rather than a juddering tug-of-war. A reel's mechanical drag system is the easiest way to facilitate this. It pays out line while maintaining the right level of tension: too much and a strong fish will snap the line, too little and the hook can slip out as the connection slackens.

But aged eight, on my first day of Spey casting, with the first sea trout I have ever hooked myself, I have no notion of this balancing act, no concept that there must be give as well as take. My brother Marcus and godfather Adrian have scrambled down the bank in response to my hollering and try to help me as the rod bulges in my hands and strands of hair fall across my face.

'Let it run,' Adrian is saying. He has grabbed the net, ready to help bring the fish in. But I am not listening. All I can feel is the line straining and all I can do, the classic beginner's mistake, is meet force with force. Rather than using my reel to pay out slack, I clamp down hard on the line in my hand, sealing it against the rod's cork handle. Quickly the line bulges until the tension tugging at my arms becomes almost unbearable. I am pulling as hard as I can, but so is the fish I have hooked, and there is only one way for this to end. Suddenly, the leader – the material that connects fly to line – snaps. All tension evaporates. The sea trout swims off and the unerring calm of the water's flow reasserts itself. I have lost the first anadromous fish I ever caught on the fly.

It is a hot, crushing disappointment and for the rest of the day I feel like a failure. But it is also the day that I become an angler.

As the baby salmon emerges from the redd it is known as a fry, and is one of the river's most vulnerable creatures. Still no more than a few centimetres long, it has now developed the outer anatomy of a fish, with fins and tail. But it is not a strong swimmer, and is not yet equipped to fight the river's current.

To reach this point, it must take its next leap of faith. With faint flutterings of its tail, the fry propels itself towards and then above the water's surface. It inhales its first gasp of fresh air. And in doing so it inflates the swim bladder, the internal organ that allows it to maintain and regulate buoyancy.

This first exploration outside the water is an adventure almost as significant for the fry as its recent hatching. After, it returns to the safer ground of the riverbed, newly capable of fighting for its place in the aquatic ecosystem – of resisting the vagaries of the current and everything that lives in it.

The fry are now self-reliant in the water's jungle, but this new-found independence comes at a cost. Their departure from the redd brings them into the realm of predators, the first of many they will encounter on the long journey ahead. They are now vulnerable to larger fish, river otters, and birds like the kingfisher that live by the river and feast on its inhabitants. As fully fledged members of the river's ecosystem, the fry are now exposed to the unsparing realities of its food chain.

The dangers are not only from other species. Fry are also a threat to each other, competing for food as they grow by feeding voraciously on plankton in the water. Those that do not fall victim to predators are equally likely to perish through starvation. These twin threats mean that the fry stage is the most deadly time to be a salmon – only one in five will survive it.

The minority that see out this treacherous first year of life become parr: juvenile salmon that have entered their penultimate stage of freshwater development, which will last one or several years and culminate in their departure from the river. At this formative point, the parr mature in multiple ways. They grow rapidly, thanks to a diet that now includes aquatic insects. They become territorial, seeking out shallow waters where larger rocks provide protection not only from predators but also from their fellow salmon. And they change their appearance, developing dark vertical bars – parr marks – that help them to blend in with, and shelter within, their chosen patch.

Although a parr has overcome so much already, it has tasted just a fraction of the dangers it will soon have to contend with. As it matures to the next stage of the salmon's life cycle, it will shed its protective parr marks, but the survival instinct they represent will remain permanently imprinted.

One thing you learn early on in fishing is that the salmon is different. The king of fish is the one that many fly anglers spend the whole year thinking about catching, willing the new season to arrive so they can resume the pursuit. This quest is defined by the enigmatic qualities of the salmon, a fish that no longer needs to feed once it has returned to the river, meaning that, unlike the trout, it is hard to tempt with the fly as a potential next meal. The salmon is not just wary; it is a fish with survival deeply encoded into its nature. A creature that has completed an extraordinary journey of migration across thousands of miles of ocean, through the worst that nature and mankind can throw at it. All this shapes the salmon, in both body and instinct, into one of the most intelligent and elusive fish an angler will encounter in fresh water. She has overcome too much to surrender lightly now. It makes every catch of a salmon unlikely; every battle with it an epic.

Before I knew or understood any of this, I was conscious of the particular way my parents talked about salmon, a detectable focus and tension when we were fishing for them rather than trout on those Scottish summer holidays. I watched my mum and dad, and I knew I wanted to emulate them, to catch a salmon for myself so I could understand why they felt so strongly about one fish that – to my young eyes – didn't look so different from the others.

Three years had passed and we were back in Scotland, this time fishing the Oykel, one of the five Kyle of Sutherland rivers, smaller and less daunting than the Spey. In stretches of the Oykel I could cast over to the other side, even at age twelve. Daintier still was the Borgie, a tiny river where – several years later, on a solo trip with my mum – I learned that being able to see a fish does not mean that you will be able to catch it. On one afternoon of pure frustration, I watched salmon after salmon jumping out of the low-lying water, flashing their middle fins at us, happy to engage in acrobatics but apparently unwilling to take the fly. The fact I could cast over them, and knew exactly where to aim the fly, made no difference: when a salmon is not interested, there is nothing you can do. I got more and more impatient until my mother finally, quietly said that she was going to move upriver to fish. 'I'm staying here,' I retorted, not taking my eyes off the water.

These holidays ran like another river through my childhood, constant but also evolving, always a different location with the nuances that every river contains. They carried on through and after my parents' separation when I was eleven, which had dispersed our family; my father remaining in our home in Stow-on-the-Wold while my mother returned to her fishing roots in Scotland. I followed her, going to school in the Highlands and splitting my summer holidays between the Cotswolds and the Scottish salmon-fishing heartlands. By my mid-teens my mother and I were making some of these trips together, but our main summer outing would still be as a family, even long after my parents had separated. They did everything they could to give us that continuity despite the distance and I never stopped feeling the love and support of both parents – their constant example, and gentle encouragement made me feel like I could bring any problem to them, and I often did.

It was fitting that both were with me on the Oykel, when I was eleven and my connection to the salmon was truly forged. I could fish on my own by now, with a beginner's deliberateness, learning how to make the line curl the way it should, and how to send the fly where I wanted it to go. The right notes, in the right order, but not yet with the serene rhythm, the almost unconscious flow, that is the mark of true casting. That would come later – much later. The subtleties of playing a fish on the line, and the patience required even during short stints on the riverbank, were becoming more familiar. But a salmon still eluded me. And the impatience that I would learn to recognise as both friend and enemy was stalking me. My parents caught salmon all the time and my brother had also landed his first. I couldn't accept being the only one to miss out.

I was fishing downstream, standing just inside the water in my thigh waders, my beloved Border terrier watching from the riverbank. She was my sidekick, following me everywhere and sleeping in my bed, her mass of coarse fawn-coloured fur pressed up against my feet. I could not have imagined life without her because she was always there, short legs struggling to keep up but never tiring.

I remember thinking that the rod was heavy and every cast felt like an effort, but I didn't want to complain, to give any hint that I wasn't capable. And then came the tug on the line, no less thrilling than it had been that day on the Spey three years earlier; the same feeling of surprise spiked with fear. A fear made so much worse by the memory of that day, the knowledge that everyone had seen me fail and that now all eyes would be on me again. *It's going to come off, it's going to come off.*

I knew that the salmon was a doubly slippery adversary for the angler: less inclined than a trout to take the fly, for it is not typically looking to feed in fresh water; and a more committed fighter, its arsenal of turns, twists and jumps constantly threatening to dislodge the hook you have set.

And I had not just hooked into any salmon. This was a grilse, a juvenile at the peak of its strength that has returned home having spent only a single year out at sea, where others will remain for two or three and sometimes even longer. A grilse may have matured more quickly than the average salmon, or perhaps encountered excessive competition for food that compelled it to return. All I knew was that this one was fighting me hard, speeding away with the fly in its mouth, its head bucking out of the water. The thrill at having hooked into a salmon was instantly tempered by the fear that I would lose it.

Part of me was terrified, thinking only of what it would feel like to let this chance slip. But I was also ready to do as I had been taught: keep tension on the line, just enough, remain content to pay some out before acting on the urge to reel in. I had my prize.

As I brought in my first salmon, the ghillie, Alisdair – Attie – who, minutes before, had shown me where to put my fly so it would swoop efficiently through the water, leaned forward to net the fish. My dog rushed up to inspect the catch, leaning her wet nose over the net but knowing better than to do anything more.

Attie smiled, his silver-grey hair the same colour as the salmon. 'Now, Marina. On this river we do what is called catch and release. We put most of the fish we have caught back into the river. But as this is your first fish, you are allowed to keep it if you want.'

I knew that keeping meant killing. Catching the fish was one thing, and something I had desperately wanted. Feeling its vigorous bite on the line and keeping it there had been a pure thrill, like little fireworks being set off all through my body. But as I looked at the fish in my net and its sleek, shimmering body, hints of pink and brown starting to intrude on its silver skin, I did not know whether I could bring myself to harm it. I didn't know, though if this was something I was supposed to do, if I would fail the test if I told Attie I wanted to put it back.

My voice was unusually quiet. 'What should I do?'

His was steady. 'I don't know, Marina. It's your choice.'

I kept looking at him but his face told me nothing. I turned to my mother and was met with the same answer.

'It's your choice.'

Then I looked at my dog, still guarding the net, not taking her eyes off the fish for a second as it gently shuddered in the shallow water. I was not afraid of the idea of a fish's death. When I was five a fisherman had killed and gutted a fish in front of my brother and me, holding up its still-beating heart in front of our small, disbelieving eyes. In Scotland we sometimes went out on a boat to catch fish to be sold at the market in Kinlochbervie, piling up dozens of pollock, mackerel and cod in crates. And I had seen my parents kill and keep plenty of the fish they caught, bringing them home to cook. I knew what it meant for those creatures to die, and I knew where my food came from. But still I wavered.

My salmon looked so peaceful in the net, compact fins giving no hint of the extraordinary journey that had brought it to this point. My decision was made.

My voice was clearer now: 'We'll let it go.'

I thought I saw Attie's smile return as he moved the net back into deeper water and beckoned me forward. With both our hands on the fish, we held it in the water, feeling its body start to buck left and right, strength returned and purpose renewed. We released it, a final few swishes of the tail, and it was reclaimed by the obscurity of the water, bidden by the need to continue its upstream journey to wherever it may end. I thought if there was a test then perhaps I had passed it.

Having released the fish, my only trophy of the day was a photograph. I still have it: I am holding the heavy double-handed rod, wearing a camo midge net and a huge pair of my mum's sunglasses. My dog is by the net, while the grilse rests on the water, right by the rocky bank. I am smiling, a little self-conscious but unable to conceal my delight that I have joined the club of people who can say they have caught an Atlantic salmon on the fly. Not long after, I hooked my second salmon. Is salmon fishing truly this straightforward? Those two fish would then return to the river, towards their unknowable future, while my own journey was becoming a little clearer. I was a salmon angler now, and I already knew that two would never be enough.

Chapter 2

Mauao or Mount Maunganui, Bay of
Plenty, Aotearoa New Zealand.

'Let's go down to the river.'

In New Zealand's Bay of Plenty countryside, I was living a life I could hardly have imagined when sitting A levels the year before. From our house perched high on a hill I could look down and see the kiwi fruit orchards stretching out below, foliage clumped together like hedges in a maze. Down the hill, crunching through clover, I quickly reached what was called the river, which was in fact not one body of water but two. On a nook of land that was washed warm by the morning sun, a stream running at the base of the hill met the river that rushed at a right angle through the neighbouring fields. At this junction of narrow and wide courses, vivid and pale blue water, meandering brook and purposeful current, we would gather: A, the boyfriend who had turned my one-month stay into something more permanent, and his friends, a gaggle of long hair, bright teeth and surfer swagger – in every sense a world away from the boys I had known growing up.

Here whole days seemed to pass when nothing really happened, but I knew this was the time of my life: in the throes of my first serious relationship, in a place where I could look out and see only green, and where mornings meant riding our neighbour's horse down by the water, pausing to run my hand through the stream's chilly turquoise. Later I would learn that this is the distinctive colour of water that has melted and flowed down from distant glaciers; light scattering off the minuscule particles of rock that the ice sheared away from its foundations as it fell. I was only nineteen years old but seemed to have stumbled into a version of life that could have been scripted for me.

Weekend afternoons, my personal idyll would become a rallying point for A's friends to cook, drink, play music, hang out and, almost as an afterthought, to fish. I was learning that, in an outdoors culture, fishing was not something that you necessarily went out to do but happened almost by default; there would usually be a rod or two lying on the grass, and we were always near the water. You cast a line because it was there, to see what happened, as unthinking as pulling the tab on the next can of beer.

While the boys chucked out spinners – weighted hooks with lures designed to rotate in the water, creating a disturbance and flash of colour to agitate the fish into a response – I often found myself hanging back. In my mid to late teens my childhood fascination with fishing had started to drift. On the most recent holiday with my mum in Scotland, she had to persuade me to spend a few hours with her on the riverbank, when what I really wanted to do was get on the train to see my friends. And in New Zealand, as a pale English girl among tanned surfers who seemed to have been born to live outdoors, I didn't want to put myself forward, to make my technique the centre of the mostly male group's attention.

Instead I stood back a little, watching A laugh as he jockeyed with one of his friends, trying to grab the fishing rod off him. Earlier that day someone's speculative cast had actually landed a fish, almost unheard of in this spot where we had now been gathering for months. A plump, quivering brown trout had emerged, its jaw gaping as if in surprise that it had found itself in such an unlikely place. Now the talk was that one must bring two, and A was determined not to be outdone. As the play-fight ended and he wrestled the rod clear, he looked round to me, checking that I was there, that I was watching.

The other people, the chatter and the laughter, seemed to fade as I watched him fish, flicking the spinner into the glistening water, with the confidence bordering on cockiness that I had loved about him from the first day he told me that he was taking me on a date. Ever since, he had been setting the pace of the relationship and I had been only too happy to follow. I had no second thoughts. In the warm sun, by that glacier-cold water, I could have sat and watched him for ever.

The juvenile salmon may remain in its birth river for several years before attempting to migrate. The parr has become a fiercely independent creature, swimming, feeding and surviving alone. Before it is ready for the rigours of the ocean journey, it must undergo an adolescence that will see the young salmon emerge as a smolt, a still-juvenile fish but with profound physical and behavioural differences.

Visibly, the camouflaging parr marks on its flanks will be replaced by the salmon's characteristic silvery sheen, itself a form of camouflage. The way the light reflects off the silver surface of the skin interferes with the distinctive ability of many sea creatures to detect polarised light, creating a mirroring effect that masks the salmon's presence and movement. The smolt's evolving camouflage is completed with the darker, light-absorbing shade that covers its fins and back. As it gets ready to swim in ocean waters, it is also preparing itself to hide in them.

Below the skin's surface many other changes are afoot. The smolt's organs must also adapt to cope with the transition from fresh water to salt water. Its kidneys adjust to produce less urine, and require less water to be ingested. The cells that line its gills prepare to switch from actively pumping sodium and chlorine into the bloodstream in river conditions, to the opposite process when the salmon encounters the ocean's salt water. As the smolt undergoes these changes, it grows longer without becoming proportionally heavier, creating a streamlined shape optimised for the thousands of miles of swimming that await.

Remarkably, the smolt also knows to lay the groundwork for its eventual return, which could be several years later. The young fish internalises the particular smell of its birth river, through a process known as olfactory imprinting. Although exactly how the salmon is able to find its way back is still somewhat mysterious, this sense of smell is likely one of the primary cues used by salmon to find their home river. In the same way as our teenage experiences are said to have a defining influence on our personality and outlook later in life, it is at this formative stage that the salmon acquires knowledge that will prove essential in the future stages of its migratory journey.

All these developments in the body of the smolt lead to one significant change in its behaviour. For most of its life so far, the salmon has been a loner, guarding its territory from peers as well as predators. But the journey ahead is too great and too perilous to be pursued alone. When warmer temperatures and longer days prompt the smolt to finally leave its home waters, it gathers with others in a large group – a shoal – in the river's lower reaches. It will commence the great adventure of its life in the same way it began in the redd: as one of many.

If New Zealand felt like paradise, it was also a form of exile from home at a time when I wasn't entirely sure where I belonged or should go next. Home was in the Cotswolds, school had been in Scotland, and now many of my friends were migrating to London. I had grown up being told that I needed to go to university, but had no real enthusiasm to take up the offers I'd received for a degree in graphic design. In my uncertainty, travel felt like the obvious answer. Most of all, I wanted to return to New Zealand, which I had fallen in love with during a school exchange trip several years earlier. I then planned to travel up the east coast of Australia and visit Thailand.

Moving around held little fear for me, since I had been doing it my whole life. My father was a property developer and we moved house frequently; half a dozen times before he and my mother separated, and several more when I was in my teens, though we rarely went very far. I would visit friends in the homes they had always lived in, wondering what it might feel like to grow up in the same surroundings, while my own were constantly changing.

Our family was loving and tight-knit even when it had dispersed to different ends of the country, but there was no denying the reality of my parents' separation. It meant always being conscious of the place you *weren't* in, as much as the one you were, pining for my old friends from home during the long Scottish school terms, then missing my mother and the Highlands when I was back in Stow.

My parents were both wonderful people but, even aged ten, I knew they were better apart. I had understood with cold certainty that it wasn't possible for two people to disagree that much and be happy together. Yet there were days when I wished they had stayed married, when I stopped understanding and felt angry that they had failed. I knew my brother Marcus, who was two years older than me, felt it too, but we spent much more time bickering than we ever did talking about what had happened. At schools in different parts of the country, we were often apart from each other as well, and when together we rarely spent much time talking about our feelings. Doing things always felt better than debating them. The unspoken family mantra was clear: *Don't complain. Ignore and carry on.* An independent streak was an inevitable consequence, and it has never gone away.

This desire to do things for myself meant that, when I needed to find work to fund my travel plans, I didn't hesitate in taking myself, straight after school ended, to London, a place I had hardly visited until then. Living in a family friend's spare room, I was free for the first time in my life to make my own decisions.

I took advantage of my freedom. After some tentative outings with school friends to preppy bars and clubs where the dress code and drinks prices told me I would never belong, I found the places where I actually felt at home: the drum and bass clubs of London's less fashionable postcodes. I loved to dance, letting the beat drive every self-conscious thought out of my head, not caring that my hair was a mess and my feet were numb, not having to think about what to say or do next. As a child I had hated crowds, but now I craved the darkness of the busy dance floor, the closeness of people whose names I would never know, the light and sound that drowned out everything on nights that seemed to go on for ever.

I went out so often it was how I found the job I had come to the city for. 'I've got an interview,' I told my mum over the phone – news she had been waiting to hear. What I didn't tell her was how it had come about: at a bar around 2 a.m. as my friend Max, so tall that he had to lean almost down to his waist so I could hear him over the music, told me about his job at a hyper-trendy shop. 'You should totally work there. I'll get you an interview.'

A few days later, trying to look perkier than I felt, wearing a pink strappy top that was actually my mother's, I was standing in a line for a group interview. One by one we were asked why we'd chosen our outfits, how we would define our personal style. Talking to Max afterwards, I found out that the girl in the pink top had been one of those chosen. Relief flooded me. I had been feeling immense pressure to get this job, fearing that I wasn't good enough. But now, I was determined to make the most of this opportunity.

The joy of this success was soon snuffed out by the reality of what my new job involved. The dark shop floor and the incessant thumping music seemed to be mocking me for all the nights I was going out dancing, as if a finger on the monkey's paw had curled and decreed that, if I really loved nightclubs this much, then I should be condemned to spend the daylight hours in one as well. Each morning there was a uniform check to ensure that our clothes were just so, there were instructions about where and how often to spray perfume on and near the clothes, and we were given stock phrases to use with customers, with a clear directive to focus attention on the obviously attractive people who fitted the 'look'.

It felt like being back in school: if you arrived wearing too much make-up you'd immediately be sent to the cloakroom to remove it. Within hours of starting, I knew that I hated it there. I didn't have the confidence to swan around as if I was better than everyone else, or the desire to find my place in the cliques that existed among my new colleagues. Instead I spent my time trying to hide in dark corners, folding t-shirts and hoping to be noticed as little as possible.

One morning the fate I had been dreading arrived. 'Rail,' the manager said when she came to my name on her list. I knew what this meant: the most public and excruciating duty in the shop, an entire shift spent up on the mini balcony at the front, dancing alongside a male colleague. I loved to dance, but here the anonymity of the dance floor was stripped away, and the joy of letting my body move drained completely as we bopped around, exposed to every pair of eyes that entered the shop, whether to leer, glance up in sympathy or simply look right through us. Reduced to human wallpaper, I struggled to keep the mandatory smile on my face as the hours crawled by. I needed money, but not this badly.

At night I partied harder than ever, trying to shake off the humiliations of my job. My family were concerned: I was becoming hard to get hold of and flaky. One night I fell asleep on the bus, waking up miles from home with no idea where I was and no battery on my phone. I stumbled through streets I had never seen before, heels clattering and hands constantly pushing up the straps on a dress that had not been designed for long walks. 'You shouldn't be alone at this time of night,' a man said as I passed. I put my head down and walked on as fast as I could. Eventually I found a tube station, slumping down outside until people came to unlock the heavy metal grilles and the first commuters of the day arrived, hi-viz jackets mixed in with the occasional business suit. Most ignored me but, once I had got onto a tube and taken off my heels, one older woman did crouch down in front of me, taking in my dress, the shoes I was holding and the mascara that stained my face. She smiled gently when I hoarsely insisted that I was ok. As she patted my hand and got up, I imagined the look on my mother's face if she could see me like this.

On another occasion, I was unsteadily following a friend across the dance floor, trying to squeeze through the gap he was opening up in the crowd, when I felt a sharp tug on my hair. Suddenly I was on the floor, two much larger girls leaning over me, punching and clawing. The crowd instinctively formed into a circle round us. I thought I could see my friend's face among them, and wondered why he was just standing there, why all these people seemed frozen in place, as if watching from another room. I didn't know what I had done – a misplaced heel or a brush past that felt like a shove? – only that they were not going to stop and I had to get away, crawling through pairs of legs until I could find the space to stand and run in the direction of the door.

Looking at my face in the mirror that night, not just cuts but little dents that showed where fingernails had dug in, bits of my hair torn out and a bruise growing on my forehead, I knew I could not show up for work the next day, or the one after that. When the store manager called a few days later, asking why I was not yet back, the coldness of her tone angered me more than anything I'd had to do while working there. 'I think I won't come in again,' was all I could manage to say over the phone before hanging up. At the time I thought it was merely a setback, but in reality my London adventure was coming off the rails, and would end sooner than I expected.

A few weeks later, it was my brother's twenty-first birthday and I was due back at my dad's house in the Cotswolds for dinner with our extended family. The plans had been in place for months. I'd been warned not to be late and a taxi had even been booked to make sure I didn't miss my train. The day came and I was up and about, checking my bag by the front door. Ready to go, I lay down on the bed, just for a moment.

As I lifted my head, I wasn't initially sure it had really happened. I couldn't have fallen asleep for long, surely. Not today. But the slight stick in my eyelashes and my desperate craving for a cigarette told me that it must have been hours. A glance at my phone confirmed the fear that was starting to twist through every corner of my body. Dad: six missed calls. Several more from an unknown number. And then the time: late, far too late to do anything, less than an hour until I was meant to be arriving with the other guests, more than three hours of car and train journeys away. I had lain down just for a minute and then slept through all those calls, through the doorbell rings from the taxi driver, through any vestiges of my body clock telling me I needed to be elsewhere.

I thought of the empty seat at the table and the look on my mother's face. The quiet excuses made. That's a pity. These things happen. Not the end of the world.

I had failed in a way that would never entirely be forgotten. It seemed to confirm every difference between my brother and me, right back to childhood when he had eked out his sweet ration over the course of the week while I gobbled mine down in one go: Marcus was reliable, sensible and trustworthy, while I was impulsive, headstrong and with a tendency to self-sabotage.

Then the phone in my hand started vibrating and I knew I could not delay the reckoning any longer. Knowing what was coming, I rushed to speak first.

'I'm so sorry.'

'Where are you?'

'I fell asleep. I'm so, so sorry. I'm going to—'

'Don't. Don't come. It's too late.'

His voice was coldly angry without being raised even a whisper above its normal level. Then a long pause. I could hear my father breathing and wondered if he could tell that I was crying. For several seconds we stayed silent, heavy with his disappointment in me and mine in myself.

'Come tomorrow. I'll pick you up at the station.'

He rang off without saying goodbye.

Almost worse than the sleepless hours that followed was the train journey itself the next day, every field that flashed by taking me closer to the conversation I was dreading. I hadn't been able to stop myself from smoking furiously that morning even though I knew my dad hated it, so much so that he had promised my brother and me money on our eighteenth birthdays if we refrained from lighting up until then: needless to say Marcus had collected and I had not. Smoking was such a big part of my life then, but on that penitent train journey the taste felt ugly in my mouth for the first time.

Throughout my life, I always knew my dad had my back and would support me in difficult moments, even if he was angry. There was no disappointment, no frustration, no questions about why, for example, I couldn't match my brother's flawless academic record. He recognised the moments where I most needed his support and comfort. This was one of those, but on that train journey I feared that I had finally pushed his patience too far.

When we pulled into the station, not even a minute late, I saw him waiting on the platform, coat zipped tight against the cold winter afternoon. For a moment we paused in front of each other, as if neither was sure who should speak first or what needed to be said. It had been a few months since we had seen each other and I was not, in any sense, the same person. I could feel him looking me over and his face softening into concern as he took in how thin I was, evident even under my thick grey fleece jacket. He opened his arms to hug me. Almost no words were spoken on the way to the car or the drive home.

The conversation I had been dreading didn't come until we were sat round the kitchen table that evening. In fact, it had already happened in my absence and I was simply being served with the conclusion.

'You're not going back to London.'

By this point arguing would have been futile, but I also knew that they were right. It was getting harder to recognise myself, or to know what I hoped to achieve by staying in the city for much longer. I couldn't carry on being the person who woke up wondering where I was and how I had got there.

The next day we booked my flight to New Zealand: a place I already loved and to which I had longed to return ever since my first visit. I was only meant to stay for a month, but it would be much longer before I saw home again.

I'd had boyfriends before, but A was different. Sitting on the beach, with only the distant mountains for company, I was watching the sun drain out of the day, long shadows dancing as A showed off for me on his surfboard, dark hair damp against the shoulders of his wetsuit. I had no idea that a man could look at me the way A did. Like I was the only thing that mattered.

I had not been looking for a relationship, but one had found me with an unnerving ease that I struggled at first to trust. One minute A was a friend of a friend, a glamorous surfer two years older than me, with whom I had exchanged a handful of Facebook messages. The next he was turning up to collect me in a green pick-up truck, looking like an extra from the episodes of *Home and Away* I had watched obsessively at school in Scotland.

Other relationships of those years had been transient and transactional – getting together with someone because everyone else was pairing up. Being cheated on by boys who would then ask you to take them back. A merry-go-round of hormones and teenage hierarchies. I knew immediately that A wanted and would give me more.

Still, I was sure he would lose interest. That I was a novelty from the other side of the world and nothing more. Yet each week, almost every day, he drew me closer into his world: soon I was meeting his big, friendly and disconcertingly beautiful family on their kiwi fruit and avocado farm, being welcomed into raucous meal-times and spending the evenings on the veranda outside, which stretched all round the white clapboard farm-house. In the dwindling light we would settle into quiet but intense conversations, holding hands as I let him tell me again and again how much he wanted me to stay.

Just weeks into our relationship I was invited to attend his sister's wedding, on the lawn outside the house, where we later camped out. In my floral halter dress, purchased specially because I had nothing suitable in my holiday wardrobe, it was impossible to stop my mind from wandering to a day in the future when we might be married here, too. We went to sleep in our tent talking, as we did most nights, about the future and how we could spend it together. As the weeks passed, I kept pushing back my flight to Australia just a little longer.

If becoming part of A's life meant sacrificing parts of mine, I felt sure it was a price worth paying. I had already let down some friends who I was meant to go travelling with in Thailand, and now I faced up to the possibility of a relationship that might not only disrupt my travel plans, but reshape the next stage of my life. I started researching ways to do my degree in Waikato and applied to a local college. I already had a job, working in a bakery, and soon I would begin my studies in graphic design. A life in New Zealand, the country I had loved so much on first encountering it that I wondered if I had been born in the wrong place, was moving from idle daydream to serious possibility.

One hurdle remained: to tell my parents, asking their permission without risking the possibility that they would withhold it. I knew that my mum's response would be to ask if I had checked with my father, so I called him first. I had been agonising for days over what to say, how to bat away the potential objections and convince him that this was what I wanted, so much so that it was worth giving up everything else I had planned. I should have known that he wouldn't be surprised by my bombshell; somehow he had always seemed to be one step ahead of wherever I was moving. He let me stumble through my script – how I knew it was a big step, but I would always regret it if I walked away from a relationship that felt so right. At the end of it, he simply asked,

'How sure are you?'

It was my dad in a nutshell: fair, to the point, and challenging you to think for yourself. It was the right question, and I knew the answer without hesitation.

Throughout the winter before its migration, the smolt's body adapts and prepares for the necessities of the journey ahead. As springtime arrives, multiple indicators tell the young salmon that the time has now come to leave home. The river warms and rises, swelled by the melting of winter snow and ice flowing downstream. The nights, in which the juvenile salmon has done most of its swimming and feeding, shorten. For a fish that has smolted, these are the signs that there is no longer a good reason to stay in the fresh water that has reared them. Their evolving body, now more suited to salt water than fresh, is also compelling them to leave. Peer pressure too may play a role, with the downstream progress of fellow smolts providing encouragement and example.

Do they go or are they taken? It is not entirely clear whether the smolt is actively swimming out to sea, simply being carried along by a current it has stopped resisting, or if it is some combination of the two. But there is some evidence to suggest that they are moving with purpose, swimming faster than the river itself is moving. As they progress through their natal waters, moving further and further from the comfort of their spawning ground, the smolt will variously point its way forward, or protectively turn away from a particularly strong current to face the home that is drifting into the distance.

The smolt run is a team exercise for these previously solitary creatures. Although the overall migration can stretch throughout spring and summer and into autumn, the vast majority of activity is highly clustered, occurring over a handful of weeks, and with the busiest periods often measured in days. This herd behaviour is partly incidental, as smolts respond to the same environmental cues. But it is also purposeful, with the concerted movement in large numbers providing some protection against the predators that occupy all stretches of the river. The feeling of safety in numbers means that smolts tend to swim closer to the surface than prior to the migration downstream, and show a greater willingness to move during the daytime, without the cover of darkness to which they previously clung.

The choice of when and how to begin their migration is another example of the salmon's extraordinary need and ability to adapt to circumstances – including those it is yet to encounter. While the conditions around them may provide the catalyst to migrate, the salmon must also intuit what the ocean water hundreds of miles away will bring when they reach it. Arrive too early and their intended prey will not have had the chance to develop sufficiently. Too late and they may have missed the best that their feeding grounds have to offer. These salmon must time not just a departure, but an arrival into an ecosystem where their standing will be even more precarious. They must anticipate what an environment they have never experienced may bring.

The smolt begins its migration prepared in some important ways for what lies ahead, but with no conception of what it will encounter in the sea. The odds are stacked against it: fewer than 1 per cent that set out on this journey will ever complete it. The juvenile salmon is relying on its extraordinary evolutionary abilities – a combination of instinct, genetic programming and herd mentality – to cling to that minuscule chance that it will ever go home again.

It all started with someone he had never met, who was thousands of miles away from us.

'Who are you texting?' said A.

'Nick. My friend from London. You know, who I was meant to go to Thailand with.'

'What are you saying to him?'

'I'm just asking how he is. Look.'

I handed A my phone, watching those familiar big eyes narrow as he scrolled.

'What the hell. Why are there *kisses* on these? That isn't friends.'

Before I could respond he had tossed the phone onto the sofa and walked out. I heard the door of our house, the haven on the hill where we had only recently moved, slam.

I told myself that it was nothing: it had been a long day. It was natural for him to have questions about my friends, given I knew all of his quite well and he none of mine. Perhaps things were just different here.

I was sure we would make up later and move on, but a seed had been planted and neither of us seemed capable of stopping that first argument from sprouting into many more that resembled it.

Every row made me a little less certain of myself: unsure whether he wanted me to tell him more about my past, which only led to more suspicious questions, or not to – and to seem evasive.

While I tiptoed from one day to the next, his behaviour became more and more distant.

We were both so young, younger than we really knew, and we argued in that way: tossing accusations at each other, propelled by our insecurities, with no concept of what resolution might look like. We were seemingly in a deeply involved, intertwined relationship, but we were not mature enough to provide the mutual support and understanding that such a partnership requires. Instead we simply found ways to like and trust each other less. There was little forgiveness, scant understanding and, as the months ticked by, less and less kindness. Each week seemed to bring something new that would feed the rising antipathy between us.

Watching my first real love sour like this would have been hard enough even if I hadn't been so isolated. When we first moved into the countryside, half an hour's drive from the city, it had felt like a dream come true: living by the water, surrounded by animals, able to pick kiwi fruits from the orchard for breakfast. We had a cat and a black Labrador, and our neighbours even sent over a couple of beef cattle to graze in our field.

Yet as our relationship narrowed into a single stream of arguments, the paradise I had been basking in felt more and more like purgatory. There was no one – not his friends or family, nor mine – that I felt able to confide in. I spent hours and hours there alone, with nothing to do except replay the previous day's argument over and over in my head. Calling home, my mother's voice faint on the phone, feeling unable to tell her the full truth of what was going on, just made me feel lonelier.

On some days I convinced myself that I could fix our problems and that we could return to how it had been. Like the gambler doubling down at the roulette table, I worked to turn things round.

I cooked, baked, and packed his sandwiches to take to the various local farms he worked on every day, trying to anticipate his every need, trying to get things back to the way they were. But nothing I did or said made a difference. The harder I tried, the more he seemed to recoil. I would sometimes walk into our house and find him sitting in the darkness, face only visible via the light of his laptop screen, not even looking up to acknowledge my presence. Sometimes after arguments he would go into our bedroom, where I could hear him punching things: when he went out I would take in how my dream house and everything it represented now seemed fractured beyond repair.

The question slipped out while I was picking kiwi fruit at the orchard. Before he had a chance either to apologise for that morning's argument or to resume it, I heard the words coming out of me.

'Do you still love me?'

He looked at me, face blank.

'No. I don't think so.'

I was so shocked that I actually laughed. Such simple devastation.

I should have left that day but I didn't. Some dogged part of me refused to let this go. Not long afterwards I spent an entire afternoon cooking an elaborate dinner, trying to communicate in one of the last ways that it seemed I had left to me. Seven o'clock, his normal return time from work, passed and I didn't dare to text asking where he was. Another hour gone and I was too hungry to wait for him any longer. Then two more hours, darkness having fallen outside, until finally I heard the door. No apology, not even an acknowledgement that he was late. Just a demand.

'Where's my dinner?'

Normally I would have made light of it, tried to soothe him. But I was angry, at having been made to wait, at how he had spoken to me, at how our hopes had withered into this miserable prison of his jealousies and my fears.

'Where's my *dinner*?' I had never seen him like this; incoherent and shaking, as if he was trying to expel every drop of emotion from his body.

I took several steps back, trying to steady my breath. 'Either you apologise right now or I'm going.'

'I'm not going to apologise.'

We stared at each other, for several long, knowing seconds. Then I heard our bedroom door slam and the familiar sound of something being thrown against the wall.

I didn't have anyone around to spell it out for me: that the relationship was dead, beyond salvation. I still found the thought of its failure intolerable – having committed so much and come so far, the prospect of leaving and admitting that it had all been for nothing somehow felt worse than the stress of staying.

But a breaking point was coming, and it finally arrived when his cousin came to stay with us a week or two later. Another furious row broke out, nothing we hadn't shouted at each other before, but for the first time it was witnessed by someone else. After I went outside to compose myself, his cousin followed. 'I'm sorry,' he said. 'I've never heard a guy speak to a girl like that. Ever.'

I immediately went inside to pack my things. A calm settled as I drove myself to the city, calling on the way a friend with whom I knew I could stay. I didn't tell anyone else where I was going; I didn't want A coming to find me.

I had made my choice and was as certain I needed to leave now as I had been a year before that I wanted to stay. After seeing out the final weeks of the college term to complete the first year of my degree, I departed with few goodbyes. I left the place I loved so much, where I had thought I might spend the rest of my life, wondering if I would ever return, and if I would ever be able to live in such a beautiful place again. Throw a rock in New Zealand and you hit a river, mountain, creek, beach or field. Living there had felt like a dream, a place where you are almost obligated to be outside, as I had spent much of my childhood. Being there had seemed like all I wanted, but now I knew I had to leave. I thought that getting on a plane would put the worst behind me – I didn't know yet that leaving was the easy part.

Chapter 3

The trout lake at Syon Park, West London.

'Put it past that boulder and just let it swing.'

Normally a ghillie would be giving this advice but it was evening, after hours, and with several blank days behind me I had come back for one last go. Tom, an old school friend, traced the correct angle for me with his finger, showing where I could land the fly so that the river would do the work, sweeping it round the full breadth of the pool in a diagonal, downstream arc.

The Spey was slow and ankle-deep, its current more a whisper than a hiss, as I prepared to cast. I fixed my eyes on the pine trees opposite, tall and impassive as they stood sentry on the steep bank, the gentle wind barely ruffling them in the fading light. There was nothing else in sight, and Tom and I murmured to each other, the solitude of the setting seeming to demand peace in return.

As the ghillie had taught me on this river over a decade before, I picked a tree to align myself with, lifting the rod tip up the line of its trunk, trying even harder than normal to work quietly. No power in the first movement, just a flop of the rod, right arm crossing over left, dumping the line round me in a half-oval. Then the sweep, bringing the line up and round the spiral staircase, letting it blow out into a D-loop, a sail at full tilt, leaving only the last section of line, the anchor, resting straight ahead on the water. And finally the forward cast to deliver the fly: power with the bottom hand and steering with the top, keeping my arms short – like a T rex, as a guide once told me – knowing that to extend them as I delivered forward would threaten the all-important tightness of the loop. I pulled the lever down, bringing my rod to a stop at ten o'clock, feeling my lower arm and elbow sink into my stomach as if to apply a brake.

I had returned to the river that held some of my strongest childhood fishing memories, where I had first caught and lost a migratory fish on the fly. And I had come back to angling, which had almost disappeared from my life during my teenage years and early adulthood. On my mind were not just the preceding handful of days without a catch, but the twelve years that had passed since that day on the Oykel when I landed my first salmon, and then my second shortly after. Despite the annual trips, there had not been another since.

With cast after cast I urged myself to hit that spot beyond the boulder, no slack line to kill the momentum of the movement, landing the fly so it was ready to accept the steady embrace of the current. The familiar rhythm of the cast flowed through my arms and shoulders as I let the river absorb my efforts, waiting, hoping, not daring to expect that my luck might change. This is the cast as lullaby: where conscious thought retreats as you watch the loop taking flight behind you and the fly curving through the water, a soothing sequence of continuous circular motion, round and round. The rod becomes a paintbrush drawing shapes in the air, an endless quest to coax the line into the perfect loop.

Then it happened. My senses registered, in whatever order, the distant splash in the water, the force of the salmon's bite and the groaning of the reel, its metallic whirring breaking the pact of silence. My mind, blissfully empty only moments ago, was teeming with every thought and fear that stalks the salmon angler with quarry on the hook. Keep a tight line, enough to stop the hook from slipping from that soft mouth. But not too tight, exerting a force that can straighten the metal until it is no longer a hook at all. Let the salmon run, taking the edge off its fearsome energy, but not too far and not too long.

The force I could feel on the line and the power of the fight in the fish left no doubt that this was the Spey salmon I craved. Then it leapt out of the water and, even in the distance, with the gloom starting to descend, I could see its glint. This was not just a salmon but a 'bar of silver', a fish recently returned from the ocean and still bearing its full protective camouflage. These are the freshest, most vigorous migratory salmon: the catch prized above all else and the only kind sought in the distant days when salmon were so abundant in these rivers that anglers could afford to be picky.

Minutes later it was in the net and I was taking in its magnificent colouring, the kitchen foil flanks giving way to gunmetal grey on the back and tail. Its bulk was such that only a firm grip, one hand by the tail and another under the pectoral fin, allowed me to hold it up for Tom to photograph. I knew without having to think that this was the proudest catch of my fishing life, one that validated all the time and enthusiasm I had poured into angling since returning to the UK from New Zealand – a second chance at making my first catch, a marker of the new beginning I desperately needed.

Only as I watched my bar of silver sinking back into the river did I take off my cap to fix my hair and realise that it was wet. So engrossed had I been in playing the fish that I had not noticed it had been raining.

The young migratory salmon has already overcome much just to reach the point where it is ready to head out into the unknown darkness of the ocean. Yet another barrier remains as the smolt reaches its departure lounge: the estuary, where river meets sea, salt water mingles with fresh water, and unforeseen dangers hover in wait.

The crossing places and meeting points of the aquatic world, estuaries are rich, vibrant, teeming environments – both nurseries and killing grounds. As filters between river and ocean, they provide a midpoint through which the migratory fish can further accustom itself to the salinity of the water, putting to its first use the body that has been adapting throughout its life so far. But they also represent a predator's habitat, partially enclosed stalking grounds for birds and sea-life to feed on the busy flows of marine traffic, from river to sea and back again.

For the smolt, which has made use of the geography of the river to survive this far – travelling at night, swimming along the bed and hiding among its rocks and pebbles – the estuary represents the most open, vulnerable environment it has yet encountered, populated by some of the most hungry predators. The young salmon has entered a new level of danger, under stress not only from the greater variety of birds, fish and marine animals that make the estuary their feeding ground, but from the effect on their bodies of the increasingly salty water, which can impede their movement and harm their ability to elude the dangers around it.

In the brackish waters of the estuary, the smolts can fall victim to other fish, including mature members of its own species, or other migratory swimmers such as cod and trout. Marine animals that will sometimes foray upstream are now clustered in greater numbers, with seals and otters among the most prevalent. The nutritious, worm-filled mudflats of the wetlands provide a home for a host of wading birds whose long legs and beaks allow them to extract insect and invertebrate prey from below the surface, but of more direct concern to the salmon are the larger birds whose hunting patterns revolve around sudden plunges into the water to scoop up an unsuspecting fish. The cormorant, one of the piscivorous guardians of the estuary, can consume more than half a kilogram of salmon in a day, and is responsible for countless smolt deaths as they pass from river to ocean.

After all it has overcome to reach this point, the smolt will experience a higher mortality rate while passing through the estuary than at any other stage of its journey leaving the river. Washed into the intermediate waters of the estuary, it is forced to confront the inescapable dangers clustered within and around. The smolt faces its moment of greatest peril yet, just as it truly begins its journey: a precipice that for many will prove to be the end of the road.

I wasn't anywhere near water when I felt the tug that would pull me back towards fishing. I wasn't in a fishing shop, although I'd started to visit those, just looking at the equipment and thinking about angling again. In fact, I was in a jeweller's, with my mother, shopping for a twenty-first birthday present. After looking at lots of pieces, we seemed to have found the one when I tried on a beautiful antique ruby ring. It fitted perfectly, the light playing off the rich red edges of the gemstone. But as expectant faces turned towards me, I felt nothing. 'Let's think about it,' was all I could manage. In reality my mind was made up. I knew there was something I wanted, but it wasn't this.

For weeks it became a running joke with my parents. 'So, have you decided?' And for weeks I prevaricated. As I turned twenty-one, trying to put the most difficult years of my life behind me, I didn't want a memento to put on my finger. I wanted something I could use. Something to do – to feel the part of myself that craves action above all else. And then my mother suggested fishing rods. The moment she did, I knew it was right and I soon agreed – two rods, a single-handed one for trout and a double-hander for salmon – the first I could ever call my own.

Though it now seems obvious – fated, even – it wasn't inevitable that I would find my way back to fishing. We were still going on family fishing trips to Scotland, but I had never struck out on my own or had my own equipment. Fishing could easily have remained the thing I did once a year, a way of spending time with my mother, a nostalgic reminder of childhood but little more.

Yet I knew that I could not go on as I was. After New Zealand, I had returned to London, choosing to complete my degree there in preference to an offer to study in Northumberland. After a year and a half of being on the other side of the world, I wanted to be close to as many friends and family as possible. I was a different person from the one who had first come to the city at eighteen, and going back held no fears. The problem was that my mind remained in New Zealand, picking at the scab of my relationship with A, wallowing in every seed of doubt he had planted. I knew that I needed help, but found I couldn't ask for it.

For my final two years as a student I pursued what felt like a double life: one part trying to dance my way through the pain, revisiting old London haunts and friendships, socialising as anaesthetic. And the other sitting for long stretches in my room alone, obsessively checking my phone, secretly still hoping to see a message from A asking me to come back.

I pursued occasional relationships, trying to recapture that addictive feeling of light-headed, light-hearted joy that had accompanied the early months of knowing A. I needed distraction but struggled to find it in a city that felt dingy compared to the life I had left behind – no last-minute plans to go surfing, no beers on the beach, watching the sun go down over the ocean. In New Zealand I had pursued an outdoor lifestyle that I thrived on and which replicated the most treasured corners of my childhood. These days I spent long periods of time sitting in a high-rise flat, gazing at the city skyline, my heart telling me that I was lost.

Indeed, my self-esteem was so low that I actually found myself pining for the relationship I had come back across the world to escape, telling friends how much I missed him on nights out, and waking up the following morning to chastise myself for my inability to move on.

Plenty of people were supportive: friends, my parents, and my brother, who frequently included me in parties with his friends and was kind and protective. As in our childhood, we didn't exactly talk about the problem, but I knew that he was trying to help me, involving me in his social life. But I also needed to talk about what had happened – was still happening – to me. Eventually, at the urging of a close friend, I went to see a therapist, and started crying as soon as she asked her first question. But I didn't commit to consistent therapy, deciding – as I so often did – that I could fix the problem on my own.

I slipped through the cracks of student life, doing the minimum required. After graduating, I continued to make myself small, abandoning graphic design and taking a job as a receptionist at an asset management company that I knew would allow me to get through the day. My fundamental confidence and ambition felt lost.

I didn't know that I needed fishing.

I wasn't aware of any part of me expressing a desire for something greater, a connection to a bigger and more meaningful world beyond the one I passed through each week. As I crossed the threshold of adulthood, my most open and vulnerable territory, I had no purpose to guide me. It seemed I was destined to simply drift.

But now I was being carried by a tide, somehow taking me to the place I needed to be. It was as if I had been searching for this missing puzzle piece that had been hiding in plain sight all along. Asking for the fishing rods was acting on an impulse; it was a feeling that would only gradually make its motivations clear. I hadn't worked any of it out yet – least of all where to store the new equipment in my tiny London flat.

But it turned out to be a pivotal event in my life, a moment whose significance I could never have realised at the time. I was now moving towards a life that would have seemed utterly, thrillingly impossible if someone had told me what was going to happen; all the places it would take me and all the experiences that lay ahead. Without knowing it, I had just taken the most important step in my life so far.

The Atlantic salmon has gone to sea not out of choice but out of necessity. It is only in the ocean that it will find the volume and variety of food it needs to grow to full size, achieve sexual maturity and move towards fulfilling the purpose of its extraordinary life: to reproduce so that its descendants may eventually follow in the same perilous journey. Because reproduction is the end to which the salmon is propelling itself, competition becomes the means. The female is preparing her body to lay as many eggs as possible into her redd, the male readying himself not just to outrun predators but to outmuscle and outshine the competition when the time comes to mate in the clear waters of the natal river.

Now, thousands of miles from home, the salmon begin in earnest the job for which they have swum so far and survived so much. As it heads north, the fast-growing post-smolt starts to feed determinedly, inhaling a mix of everything and anything that floats into their path: insects, plankton, crustaceans, molluscs and small fish. As well as consuming at the surface and immediately below, where it does the vast majority of its ocean swimming, the salmon will make occasional deep dives to hunt for less conveniently located prey. It is voracious as it passes through ocean waters, opportunistic in its feeding habits.

As the salmon feasts on the diet that the marine environment can uniquely provide, it is meeting multiple needs in parallel. The different forms of nutrition spur growth, at the same time helping it to secrete fat under the skin, a necessary store for the long return journey to the river, by which time the salmon's feeding frenzy will be over. Some of that fat is likely to oxidise into water, a precious source of hydration in the liquid desert of the ocean. In addition, it is not just ingesting nutrients but pigmentation too. The mature salmon's characteristic pink hue results not from a colour it creates itself, but one it sucks up from the ocean's currents: carotenoid, produced by algae and transferred to the fish through the fat of the creatures that consume it, which the salmon feasts on in turn.

As it does throughout its journey, the salmon is unconsciously anticipating future needs at the same time as managing present ones, feeding not just for today and tomorrow but for the rigours of the journey that lies far ahead. It carves out a slim chance of surviving that journey thanks to the remarkable evolution that urges it to develop its body not just for the challenges that immediately surround it, but also for those that lie unfathomable miles into the distance, and unforeseeable months and years into the future.

My new rod almost seemed to be reproaching me, as if it knew it had fallen into inexpert hands. Just to set up my equipment I was leaning on barely trained muscle memory, recalling how to work my way down from tip to handle, squeezing together the sections and lining up the guides – metal eyelets through which the line is fed to hold it in position. As I attached the foot of the reel to its seat on the rod, I recalled my mother's advice to pull out not one length of line but two, doubling it over as insurance in case it slips from your fingers as you thread it. I swore quietly to myself as I tied on my fly, fingers fussing over the knot, the most important part of readying the equipment and, for the novice, the most exacting. A final check: hook the fly you have tied onto the zip of a bag or jacket and pull tight. It held.

Then, with the line laid out ahead of me, fully extended onto the stillness of the lake, it was time. The rod tip lifted, as gently as possible: no fast pick-up that would disturb the surface and send the trout scuttling for cover, ending the pursuit before it had even begun. Slowly, carefully, I 'peeled' the line upward, an elbow movement bringing the tip of the rod to just above eye height. Then an acceleration of the upper arm, taking the rod back in a straight line and to a stop behind me, at 1 o'clock on the clock face. A pause, just long enough, to let the magic start to happen. The loop unrolling behind me, a fleeting display of geometry to observe from over my right shoulder. And the final action: a mirror of the backcast, bringing both rod and line sharply forward to a stop at 10 o'clock, again and again until the slack line has disappeared from my side, sending the fly onto the water – towards the spot where I saw the trout rising to the surface to feed, and where I had been watching it biding its time all morning.

These routines – the setting up of my new fishing rod and the basic overhead cast – were the rituals that defined the weekends of my early twenties as I took myself Saturday after Saturday to the closest angling spot I could find: the trout lake at Syon Park on the outskirts of West

London. Set within the grounds of the grand Syon House, the lake was originally created by the eighteenth century's pre-eminent landscape architect Capability Brown. It was here that my life in fishing was reborn.

The park was an odd vision of paradise. It was neither fully town nor country: there were cows fenced back from the lake and geese wandering the banks, with high-rise buildings visible in the distance, and the Heathrow flight path humming overhead. But at a time in my life when I badly needed something, Syon became my escape. I would show up almost every weekend, occasionally with an old school friend who was an avid angler, or sometimes dragging a non-fishing acquaintance along. But most often I was alone, my spirit rising at the thought of a day with nothing else to worry about.

Everything I needed was in the car and I would set up my equipment there. I had the simplest fishing kit: just a floating line and a small box of flies – no alternate tips or lines to experiment with. If I'd made an early start, I might be able to bag one of my preferred spots, on the right-hand side of a bridge near some trees: two physical features that provided shelter for the fish, and where I learned I could have a fruitful day casting a fly. Or if I wanted to test myself I would push on towards the top of the lake, where bushes provided the same certainty that fish would be present, but the embrace of the trees and foliage made casting more of a challenge – a careless line was liable to get tangled in the branches.

I fished so much in those days that it was starting to take over my entire life. At work I would spend idle time thinking not of beach holidays but about new places to go angling. Friends would sometimes make wry remarks about how much time I seemed to spend at the lake. Then one Saturday evening, as I was heading out to a party, I realised that I had nothing to bring with me. In a rush as I was, all I could think of was the stocked trout I had caught that afternoon, now sitting in my fridge. It was presented to my friends on the doorstep, a dripping package handed over with pride and received with polite bemusement.

I was back at the beginning: lake fishing for brown and rainbow trout, one of the simplest and most accessible forms of angling there is. This was how I had first learned to fish, near home in Stow. And now it was how I would learn to fish for myself, tracking the trout that constantly moved through the gentle water, looking for food on the lake bed, among the aquatic vegetation, in the water columns and on the surface. So much of a day just spent watching the water, searching for the rising ripple – the telltale shift against the current – that discloses the presence of a trout hiding under a bank or among leaves. Urging the lake to give me a sign: *come on, do something.*

Every Saturday was another chance to get lost in the maze of decisions that is part and parcel of the sport: where to stand, what cast to use, whether to change fly if nothing seemed to be happening. Another chance to occupy myself with the rigours of casting: a discipline that tempts, taunts and teaches you with its nuances. Enough power in the backward stroke to load the rod with energy, but not so much force that you hear the dreaded whipping noise that says you have overdone it, causing the line to cross over itself, to the point where it can literally tie itself in knots.

It was, as beginnings often are, both the best and the hardest part: when I had the most still to learn, but could also take the purest joy in every small achievement, a good, accurate cast almost as pleasing as a catch. Although I had had a few lessons, I was mostly self-taught: a slower and harder but ultimately fulfilling route, where you learn to rely on your own experience and instincts, not waiting for someone to point at a seam in the water, correct your technique, or tell you to go to that tree and cast. But it also meant long days of frustration, where I would admonish myself for not getting enough distance on the cast, and then overcompensate with too much power and lose time untying the wind knots from my line. Looking down the lake, I would wonder at how others could reel off cast after perfect cast while my own movements felt lumpy, my loops anything but tight, and the fish seemingly repelled by every fly I chose.

Then somehow the doubts would clear, the mistakes would recede and rhythm would arrive. I would know that I had given just enough time for my loop to take full flight, put the right amount of force into the stroke, and was about to be rewarded by seeing my fly soar along with my soul as it landed just where I wanted it. Sometimes such moments would not arrive until late in the day, after hours of trial and error, effort and empty nets. Still I would work away, trying to suck every minute of fishing out of the day, continuing to cast even as the sun started to dip and its warmth drained away, along with my hopes of making a catch.

On one of these blank Saturdays I knew I had, at best, fifteen minutes before I would have to walk back to my car in the dark, empty-handed. Having tried everything else, I played my last card: an orange blob fly, fluffy and Fanta-coloured, the brightest and boldest thing in my box. I hurried to tie it to the line and made what I knew would be one of my final casts of the day. On the first try it took, a trout pulling the line so hard that I almost dropped the rod in my surprise, the fish taking so well that I saw its head break through the surface of the water. Hooking into that trout did not just feel like a triumph to cap a long day's work; it made me eleven years old again, the tug of joy in my stomach matching the pressure of the fish's bite on the fly. And more than that, this joy felt *earned*, a reward for rigour and precision, a recognition of my slowly evolving technique and skills.

These days by the lake went beyond simple childhood nostalgia. They were also slowly pulling me out of the dark pool in which I had been swimming circles since my return from New Zealand. My childhood experience of fishing had shown me the excitement and the challenge that comes with angling and the pursuit of the next catch, but gave me little appreciation of how fishing can empty the mind and soothe the soul. With a rod in my hand and my mind fixed only on what was in front of me, intrusive and corrosive thoughts would subside – at first for the afternoon, but increasingly for the rest of the week as well. My anxiety would drain away, displaced by my need to watch the water, hear its music and absorb the clues that indicate where and when to cast a fly. I learned to love the simple feeling of fishing: being in an environment where nothing else matters, where the water beneath you has been flowing this way since long before you existed, and will continue to do so after no one is left to remember you.

Coming back to fishing also reminded me of my real self: someone determinedly independent, skilful with my hands, and capable of setting a course. It helped me remember what I could do and what I wanted to do, reducing the mental space to agonise further over things that had gone wrong and past decisions that could never be unmade.

My confidence was starting to grow. Before long I wanted more than the placid lake of Syon Park, and started venturing further afield with my trout rod – to Grafham Water in Cambridgeshire, where I talked a local fisherman into taking me out on his boat to fish for trout, and to the River Test in Hampshire – my first introduction to its dazzlingly clear chalk stream waters.

And when I wasn't actually out on the water, I was thinking about where I could go next, rivers I wanted to fish and techniques I wanted to experiment with. There were few times when fishing wasn't on my mind. On a hiking trip to Norway with a friend, I insisted we stop by one river because I had seen a stick that could be made into a just-about functional rod. I attached the reel that I had brought with me, even though we had made no plans to go fishing, and flicked a line onto the water. To my delight, a small brown trout emerged and took my fly.

Fishing wasn't far away even when I accompanied a friend to see a clairvoyant and decided to have my own fortune told. I drank the tea and watched the cards being dealt in front of me, sceptical that I would hear anything more than a series of conveniently vague predictions. Someone in my life was jealous of me, my then boyfriend was not the man I would marry – although this last prediction did turn out to be accurate. I was losing interest when she made one final comment. 'The main thing I see, in fact the only thing I keep seeing, is water everywhere. I'm not sure if you're in the water or travelling over it, but water is what I see.'

The clairvoyant's vision may have been approximate, but as I left the room I knew exactly what it could mean – and, more importantly, what I *wanted* it to mean. I had found the purpose that would pull me forward. I didn't yet know that fishing would become my career, but I already clung to it as a source of focus and ambition, driving an unrelenting need to improve and show I could be better. To carve out a piece of my life that I could shape on my own, and where success was in the gift of my hard work. Fishing was the perfect balance of reward and challenge, feeding both the quiet and loud sides of my personality. By then I was convinced that there were few better ways to be mindful, quell anxiety and build confidence than fishing.

At the lake I became less self-conscious, more willing to ask other anglers for help and advice, and increasingly grooved in the mechanics of my cast. Although, in my habitual impatience, I had to remind myself that I was still little more than a novice. 'You'll be a good caster,' an older man fishing near me commented on one of those long afternoons by the trout lake, grinning over his stripy polo shirt – not quite the image of the tweedy fisherman I knew so well from Scotland. The pride immediately swelled in me, before he delivered his punchline. 'If you give it another year or two.'

Knowing that it would take time to improve did not deter me, though. I was now firmly back under the water's spell, being reminded that, while the fly is there to lure the fish, in so many ways it is the angler who gets hooked, dragged further and further into the world of endless possibilities that fishing contains. Fishing is the ultimate bucket list pursuit – you will never meet a serious angler who can't talk for hours about all the places they want to go and the fish they would love to catch.

Fishing tugs you with equal force back to the waters imprinted with years of memories, and towards those which you will be experiencing for the first time. There is always another fish to pursue, another river whose nuances need to be understood, and another variation on the cast to learn. Only after you have mastered the basics can you appreciate angling's steep learning curve with its endless gradations of experience and ability. These are progressively revealed through years of practice, a spiral staircase of knowledge that simply keeps on ascending. As someone who loves to challenge themselves, to learn and to constantly move on to the next thing, it was perfect for me. Every time I packed up my equipment at the end of a day's fishing, there was only one question in my mind: where next?

CATCH

Chapter 4

River Test, Hampshire.

Alongside the salmon fishing rivers of Scotland, the chalk streams of England are the jewel in the crown of Britain's waterways. In the riffles of their aquifer-fed waters, where the flow is slow and shallow, rocks and debris provide ample hiding places, and food and oxygen are plentiful, brown trout, silver salmon and the red-fringed fins of grayling abound. These fish are not just present but visible, as the novelist Richard Adams described in *Watership Down:* 'Suddenly, from under the bridge, with a languid movement of its flat tail, swam a gravel-coloured fish as long as a rabbit. The watchers, immediately above, could see the dark, vivid spots along its side. Warily it hung in the current below them, undulating from side to side.'

Adams was writing of the River Test in Hampshire, the nation's longest and foremost chalk stream: a waterway that feels distinctly English, fringed with weeping willows, thatched cottages and an abundance of flowers, from the finger-like pink petals of ragged robins reaching out towards the sun, to the simple warmth of buttery yellow daffodils. Cut through the chalklands synonymous with the south of England, the Test feels timeless:

clean, clear, highly oxygenated water bubbling up from the chalk aquifers; its flow steady, its temperature moderate and its contents alkaline, the sediments that cloud most river water filtered away by the chalk to leave only the delicious clarity of the stream.

The serenity of the river, broad and open stretches where it rises barely above the ankle giving way to narrow, vegetation-shrouded corners, seems to match the surrounds as it flows through the Hampshire countryside – from its source in Ashe, near the birthplace of Jane Austen, past landmarks including Romsey Abbey, where abbesses held sway from the reign of Alfred the Great's son until Henry VIII's dissolution of the monasteries. One of them, Aethelflaeda, Abbess of Romsey, was renowned for bathing in the river. She is even credited with a miracle whereby the wall of the abbey supposedly turned to glass, allowing her to see through it much as she might have the gin-clear waters of the Test itself.

Over forty miles and several centuries, the Test has exercised a hold on the imaginations of authors and anglers, because of the beguiling clarity of its water and the rich density of its hatch – the early-evening moments when flies emerge from the nymph onto the surface and trout rise to feed on them. The simple joy of being able to sight-fish this river never goes away, whether you are kneeling down on naked banks to cast, eyes close to the flinty bed over which just a shallow coating of water flows, or stooped in the shade of an alder curving protectively overhead, its long roots reaching into the river to cradle both fish and fly.

Yet we should not take for granted that this beautiful, peaceful, gloriously biodiverse water will always remain so. As an iconic English river, and perhaps the most famous of all chalk streams, the Test is also a barometer. And in the decade of my fishing career, it has been swinging more and more towards widespread alarm for the state of our rivers, stressed by a combination of rising temperatures, poorly maintained infrastructure and the licence granted to water companies to release raw sewage into them – injections of pollution directly into the arteries of our natural world. Even the Test, with its high profile and protected status, is at risk, as several incidents in recent years have shown. A stretch of the lower river became polluted after diesel leaked into it in the summer of 2021, leading the Environment Agency to designate it as 'unfavourable' for wildlife. The previous year, monitoring had shown that raw sewage was dumped into the Test and its tributaries for a combined total of 4,000 hours. In 2022, Southern Water sought a permit that would have allowed it to keep drawing water from the Test even when it had fallen to dangerously low levels, an application it eventually withdrew under public pressure.

These incidents are part of a troubling picture: UK rivers under attack from a three-headed monster comprising drought, the overspill from our insufficient sewerage systems, and chemical waste from farming and industry. The same situation is mirrored elsewhere: in the US, a study in 2022 measuring almost 1.5 million miles of rivers and streams found that over half of the water was too polluted to swim in or drink from, or to support aquatic life – pollution from industries including agriculture being one of the main culprits.

The Test, one of our most cherished and famous rivers, being in trouble gives an indication of how serious the wider situation is. In common with other chalk streams, it plays host not just to a historic salmon population but to one that is genetically distinct. Numbers have already declined, and, if they continue to do so, we will lose something that cannot be replaced.

These rivers must be protected because without them so much deeply entwined wildlife will suffer and die: the plants being suffocated by algal blooms brought about by chemicals leaching into the water; the insects whose food sources are being choked off by pollution, and the knock-on effect this has on the fish that feed off them, as they suffer in turn from rising water temperatures and threats to oxygen levels. Everything is connected: these are wondrous and fragile ecosystems that will be lost unless we take the steps necessary to protect them.

Fishing the Test, a world away from the placid lake at Syon Park, took me back to the purest form of the sport. A river, with its eddying currents and untamed habitat, is a more intense and compelling experience for the angler who has begun to gain confidence in their technique. Mistakes happen more easily – the line trapped in the branches of the tree behind you, or caught in the vegetation in front – but the feeling of luring a fish from the river is unlike any other. There is a tangible sense of being in control of your actions and in tune with the subtleties and complexities of your surroundings. If I could only choose one river to remain in the world, in its untouched and wild state, it would be the Test.

I had loved coming to the Test ever since I was first introduced to it: a day of fishing its flawless waters would usually be followed by the comfort of an overnight stay with my grandparents in Stratford, in the only house I had ever known them in, the one family home that had been the same since my childhood. But this day was different. I was on the banks of the river, a rod in my hands, a trout in my sights. And a knot in my stomach that told me this would be no peaceful morning of watching the water and feeling the flow of the cast. I was here not to enjoy the Test but to be judged by it. Against this ageless backdrop, I was faced with the very pressing concern of my embryonic fishing career, and whether I had what it took to take the first step.

The more fishing I had done, the less inclined I was to keep it to myself. I wanted to share the moments of joy and relief when a long day of casting had been rewarded by a last-gasp catch. Without thinking about what I was doing, and with no plan at all, I turned to social media. My Instagram started to become an incongruous mix of party pictures and photos of trout and fly patterns. Today, I think carefully about everything I put into the public realm, but these were the early and relatively innocent days of the platform. I had no expectation that what I was sharing would go beyond my circle of family and friends, let alone that it might turn into something more.

When I posted about my bar of silver on the Spey, I started getting likes and comments from people I didn't know personally. This was the time in my life when fishing was pure obsession, all I wanted to talk or think about. And now I was finding others who wanted to do the same: fishing people who would praise the catch, wish me tight lines, ask where on the river I had caught something and what fly I had used. Soon I was posting less about my social life and more about my angling exploits. Before long I had added the word fishing to my online identity, styling myself as @marinagibsonfishing.

At a time when people were only just starting to talk about concepts like influencers, and companies were just beginning to see the value of social media in reaching new audiences, I was unwittingly becoming part of a trend. So too, in its way, was fishing. An ancient sport shapes up with surprising ease under the lens of new media. The glistening sheen of the water, the variety of the surroundings, and the beautiful detail of the fish themselves all combine to make angling an improbably photogenic and socially magnetic entity. Growing up, I had seen anglers, including my godfather, keep a long-hand fishing diary describing the ups and downs of each day on the water. Instagram became my version of that, depicting moments of triumph and days of frustration, with the added dimension that it could spark conversations and dialogue, one angler sharing tips and experiences with another – much as happens on every riverbank around the world. (There would also be a less welcome strain of online feedback, which I would only discover later as my audience grew further.)

I was enjoying this new dimension to my fishing life, but had no plan for it, no sense that it might hold the key to the thing I by now desperately wanted – to turn fishing from a hobby into a career. And then Orvis, one of the major fishing gear brands, got in touch. They liked what I was doing and might be interested in working together. Would I join them for a day they were hosting on the Test? I knew what this meant: a potential sponsorship. This was my opportunity – perhaps the best and even the only one I would get.

I moved around the U-shaped beat, working my way upstream, conscious of the organisers' eyes on me. As the morning slipped by, I threw out more and more casts but with no luck, and stress started to creep up my arm and into my shoulder. I knew that I was doing nothing wrong. My line was perfectly straight, the twinge of tension just right on the backcast as the loop took flight, horseshoe silhouette flashing through the still air as the shallow water waited. Yet each time I propelled my fly onto the surface of the river, it seemed to fall on ground every bit as stony as the flint below.

What completed my torture was that, courtesy of the chalk stream's perfect clarity, I could see every detail of the stubbornly unmoving fish I was trying to catch. Of the fish I sought that morning, one in particular became the focus of my attention. I could almost have counted the spots that ran leopard-like along the full width of its flanks, giving way to the champagne shades of its lower body. Like the rabbits of *Watership Down* I watched my fish poised effortlessly in the current, using the gentle flow to hold itself in place. It moved just enough to intercept passing morsels of food, like sushi on a conveyor belt, but it never strayed beyond its carefully guarded territory. I knew it was a 'riser' and had seen it come to the surface several times to feed. But it clearly had no intention, as minutes turned into an hour and a handful of casts became dozens, of taking my fly.

The fly: perennial source of love and hatred, discussion and obsession. Twists of thread, artificial feathers, wings and eyes round a metal hook, into which we invest all our hopes of catching a fish that day, if only we can find the right one: the fly that grabs the attention of the trout, which looks like the next mouthful it has been waiting for, compelling it to open its jaws and bite. Of all the decisions and considerations that fly fishing contains, none occupies so much time and anguish as the question of which fly to tie onto the line: small or large, subtle and stealthy, or brash and bold. By every riverbank, the debates rage and the rumours circulate about what the fish are feeding on and what has been working. Then the fishing begins and, on a blank day, two voices begin to assert themselves, the angel and the devil on the shoulder of every angler.

Stick with it.

The first thought, the one that should be right. Give it a chance, you chose this fly for a reason, don't give up so easily.

Change it.

The tug on the sleeve. You made a bad decision. It was never the right fly. Go on, try something else.

You look at your fly box, knowing that there is something in there that's a bit brighter, a bit more obvious, or a better match for the fly life you have seen. When the trout are rising to feed on flies sitting on the surface of the water, you reach for a dry fly that can replicate the insect you can see it is gorging on, be that a sedge, hawthorn, mayfly or one of the many others. If nothing is rising, a nymph – a wet fly resembling unhatched larvae that is delivered into the water

– might be the answer. Or you can try to tempt the fish with a streamer, which is pulled quickly through the water to replicate the movement of fast-moving aquatic life, and which you will 'retrieve' by stripping the line to keep it mobile. The fly box is a constant source of temptation, and the angler's art is to decide when to give in and switch, and when to hold firm for a little longer. You are forever on the verge of reaching for a different fly, while constantly telling yourself not to rush into another change.

This is a long-debated aspect of fly fishing, stretching back into its distant literature. 'The modern school are far too much addicted to continual change of fly, often changing merely for the sake of changing . . . forgetting that the fault too often lies in their own lack of discrimination,' scolded the author F.M. Halford, writing in 1889. A Victorian fly fishing authority who wrote under the amazing pen name 'Detached Badger', Halford preached the gospel of the dry fly: an artificial lure that sits on the surface of the water, which must be cast upstream behind the head of a trout rising to feed, so it would float past its eyeline as if nature, not the angler, had put it there. It was on the Test that Halford conducted much of his research into fly life and trout feeding patterns, in an obsessive quest to develop exact artificial replicas.

His influence on the river endures; on many beats only dry flies are used for much of the season, with anglers spurning nymphs and streamers. For Halford disciples, the latter two are almost cheating, too close to fishing with actual bait, and only the technical rigour of coaxing the trout to rise to take a dry fly on the surface really counts as fishing.

Being aware of this local dry-fly etiquette only added to the pressure I felt that day. I knew I was casting to get my foot in the door of the fishing industry, and how easy it would be to make a novice error in this historic setting.

Nevertheless, I ignored Halford's imprecation to avoid changing my fly. With so much at stake, it was not a day for waiting patiently. I cycled through flies, from mayfly to caddis, emergers to upwings, beetle and ant, throwing different shapes and colours at the trout, hoping that this one would magically unlock its attention, anything that might tempt it to the surface in the expectation of being able to feed. Time after time, the result was the same and I chided myself for having made yet another change, regretting each decision almost as soon as I had made it. A man in a brimmed hat, fishing on the opposite bank, kept casting inquisitive glances my way, as if curious about my every move.

Lunchtime was approaching and I could already picture myself being the only one to return empty-handed from the morning's fishing. I decided to change things up one final time. I reached for a crane fly, putting my trust in its two oar-shaped wings and six spindly legs to entice the trout. The daddy-long-legs, as it is also known, is an appealing food source for the trout and a classic Test fly. I had left it in my box because I hadn't seen a real one on the surface, and I was trying to match the pattern of what my extremely picky trout was feeding on; so it was in near desperation that I turned to the crane, an unmissably large fly that I knew would land more heavily than anything I had yet cast. Before I could doubt myself again, I was tying the knot, wetting it in my mouth to keep the line supple as I tightened it, and making the cast.

On the very first go with the crane, it happened. Smoothly, serenely, as if this had been the plan all along, my trout rose, almost smashing its head into the fly as it swallowed the hook. The line tightened reassuringly, a tension I had never been more relieved to feel. Soon that trout was in my net, body resting in the water as I let it rest and secured my proof that I could land a fish after all. A nod and a kind comment from my neighbouring angler confirmed that I had made the right impression. He even complimented me on my willingness to keep changing my fly.

A day that had flirted with disaster turned into a success. Shortly afterwards I became an Orvis ambassador, and had my first taste of working in the fishing industry. I agreed to use and talk about their kit, and to attend events during the spring and summer months of the domestic fishing season. I had a full-time job as an executive PA in London, but my mind was turning more and more to how I could make fishing as big a part of my life and livelihood as possible. I was snatching every opportunity, eager to fish whenever and wherever I could. But as my career in fishing took shape and I set out towards my dream, I would soon find that my eagerness would not always be reciprocated; nor would I always be made to feel welcome in the industry I wished to call home.

The continents of the Earth do not end at the visible boundary where land meets sea. The ground extends, submerged in the waters of what will become the deep ocean, forming what is known as the continental shelf. The shelf slopes and then, eventually, it drops, giving way to the deep floor of the open ocean. It is down this gradual then sudden escalator that the Atlantic salmon is swimming as it makes its way towards the Norwegian Sea to feed, making use of the rapid northerly current that flows through the waters of the continental shelf.

In this early ocean voyage, the salmon enjoy a rich and diverse diet, supported by the continental shelf's amply oxygenated waters . They typically travel in small shoals, convoys of fellow post-smolts that aid both direction and predator detection.

Yet alongside what we know for certain about the salmon's journey, there are mysteries – quirks of behaviour and unexplained sources of ability that power the salmon's improbable progress. The salmon's journey north takes it past feeding grounds that it sees but hardly engages with, on the way to others it cannot yet know will exist.

The salmon's focus is increasingly narrow. They press on northwards, over the continental shelf and down its slope. But how do they know where they are going? Another mystery, as yet only partially explained. A form of magnetic navigation may hold the key; this is facilitated by particles in their bodies, partly absorbed from the iron in their diet, which similarly feature in the physiology of the homing pigeon. This would explain the salmon's steady northward compass, as well as its apparent advanced ability to use the features of the ocean to its advantage.

Whether it is magnetism or sensitivity to water temperature or salinity that drives the salmon is still a matter for scientific hypothesis and conjecture. But what cannot be doubted is the relentless nature of the fish as it pilots its way through an environment so different from the one in which it was born. Compelled by evolution and conditioned by the example of those around it, the salmon continues on, as the continental shelf subsides into deep ocean, and its surroundings become ever vaster and more unfathomable.

As I made my early forays into the fishing industry, there was a look I got used to seeing: a series of expressions that would break over men's faces as I introduced myself, like one of those cartoon books you flip through with your thumb to watch the story unfold. First would come surprise: *a woman*. Then composure as they settled on an explanation: *probably shopping for her boyfriend; someone's secretary*. And finally, as I explained that the equipment would be for me, or that I was asking after job openings for myself, a realisation that landed somewhere between amusement and disdain.

These were the looks I encountered in London fishing shops and at the Game Fair, an annual showcase for country sports, which I had attended regularly with my family growing up, and was my first port of call when looking for fishing jobs. As I went from stall to stall, people took copies of my CV but didn't read them. Instead their eyes were fixed on me, looking me up and down, before turning to the person next to them, as if to share in the best joke they had seen that day: *a girl, who wants to work in fishing?*

It would be wrong to overgeneralise my experiences as a woman in fishing, because I have also received so much support and encouragement from fellow anglers at every step of my journey in the sport. Female participation in fishing is growing all the time, building on a legacy that demonstrates that women have been among the most notable and successful anglers in the sport's history. Women make up an increasing number of recreational anglers, taking advantage of clubs, events and outfitters that are specifically geared to support female participation. At the same time, angling still often lives up to its reputation for being male-dominated and unwelcoming, and this was especially true when I was first making my way. Today the sight of a woman going into a fishing shop isn't as unusual as it was in the early 2010s, let alone in the 1980s when my mother was getting serious about fishing. Women are both more active and more visible in fishing, as guides, hosts and organisers. Still, a decade later, attitudes have not entirely changed. One woman I was teaching recently told me how she had gone shopping for equipment, only to be asked if she wanted to 'go and look at the pretty flies for your husband'.

In my early days of fishing independently, taking myself and sometimes a friend to the lake at Syon Park, I was never quite sure what sort of reception I would encounter. For some anglers we were an amusing novelty. When I brought along my friend SJ, who in her leather jacket and skinny jeans had little intention of getting anywhere near a fishing rod, I noticed that a neighbouring fisherman kept looking quizzically over, perhaps wondering if she was going to have a go. He was bringing in fish the whole time and eventually, with a trout on the line, generously offered her the rod so she could reel it in.

Another such episode was less comfortable: under the guise of teaching my friend how to hold the rod, one man wrapped his arms round her and put his hands over hers to demonstrate – a complete violation of her personal space and the number one thing you shouldn't do when showing someone how to cast. But most often, people simply didn't engage with me. I would encounter men, usually older, who refused to acknowledge me next to them on the riverbank or whose conversation would be limited to a grunted monosyllable. The message felt very clear: that I didn't belong in their world.

One of the few welcoming people I met at the Game Fair was a fishing tour operator from Canada, who warned me of a darker side to these attitudes. Over a shot of 'Sturgeon Pee' – his secret stash of home brew – he offered some bracing advice: 'The thing you need to be aware of is that there are wolves in the fishing world, and you need to be careful who you work with.' I wasn't initially sure what to make of this, but my early forays into the industry showed me exactly what he meant. In my spare time and holidays from my job, I started going on fishing trips, doing bits of work for tour companies, and embarking on my first coaching qualifications with the Angling Trust. In Green Park, near my office, I set up a free once-a-week lunchtime class where people could come and learn the basics of fly fishing technique: Casting in the Park. Orvis kindly provided the equipment. It was my first experience of teaching, and I found it immensely rewarding. Even far from the water, people cast a line onto grass, I enjoyed the process of helping them to improve their technique and feel the satisfaction of getting shoulders, rod and line in sync. It was an early indicator of my desire not just to spend my own life fishing, but to persuade more people to give it a go.

Naively, I didn't seriously consider that people would try to exploit my enthusiasm and eagerness to get a foothold in fishing, but several did, and I experienced a few notable incidents of sexist and predatory behaviour. One company offered me a deal to help promote their brand, but, just as we were getting ready to announce the partnership, the owner suddenly made it clear that he wanted photographs of me wearing as little clothing as possible; I went to his online fishing shop and found he had already posted a photo of me in a bikini, ripped from my social media without permission.

On my first ever fishing tour abroad, the organiser, a man I hardly knew, emailed to say we would be sharing a room. I insisted on my own room, but when we arrived, he was unkind, constantly critiquing my technique and chastising me for losing fish. I felt nervous and rushed, so I lost more fish than I should have. We shared a boat on the water, so there was no escape. I felt vulnerable and realised I needed to be more streetwise when choosing to fish abroad with strangers.

Such incidents were the exception not the rule, but fishing was absolutely a male-dominated world. The instructor on my Level 1 coaching course with the Angling Trust laughingly remembers me as 'that nervous girl' who arrived late to the session, into a room that was otherwise populated only with men. Several years later, when I did my Level 2, the instructor was an inspiring woman, Sue, but I was still the only female student.

In frustration I would sometimes share these experiences with my mother, who would nod her head with the look of someone hearing an all too familiar story. 'Can she cast?' were the words she overheard ghillies muttering in disbelief on Scottish rivers in the 1980s. Even as a child in love with the water, she would sometimes be left behind when her brother went out for a day's fishing.

Happily, the more I have become involved in fishing, the more I have realised that I am far from alone as a female angler. I have met so many women – at fishing shows and fairs, as students at my fishing school, and on trips around the world – who have shown me that we can be angling obsessives as much as any men, and that fishing can be many things other than stuffy and tweedy.

I have made some of my best friends through fishing: women whose strong, boisterous personalities match my own, and who agree that there is nothing quite like fishing to feel both at one with yourself and together with others. Among them are 'the two Claires' – Clare B. and Claire S., the first an artist who paints using pheasant feathers and the second a corporate lawyer. But beside each other on the riverbank we feel like three versions of the same person.

It is ironic that women are sometimes made to feel unwelcome in fishing, for there is a proud history of female anglers, who have been responsible for some of the biggest and most notable catches ever achieved. In October 1922, late in the day and at the very tail end of the season, Georgina Ballantine, a Scottish nurse and daughter of a ghillie, hooked into a River Tay salmon that, with three catches already behind her that day, she expected to bring in easily. Little did she know that on the line she had a monstrous fish almost a metre and a half long, weighing in at sixty-four pounds. What she later described as a 'Homeric battle' ensued for just over two hours, as Georgina and her father hopped in and out of their boat while she played this massive fish, which ended up dragging them over a mile downstream. It remains the largest salmon ever caught with a rod in British waters. To put it into perspective, my own biggest UK salmon – also caught on the Tay – was a mere eighteen pounds. That was enough of a challenge to bring in, feeling like a millstone on my line, not moving particularly quickly but banging its head furiously, strong enough to propel itself upstream despite the pressure of my rod and line. The big ones are always a shock when you hook into them, because they sit so deep in the water you rarely see them at first. After my ghillie netted the fish for me, I tried to hold it for a quick picture before releasing it, but it was so strong that it leapt straight out of my hands and back into the river. 'My hands won't stop shaking,' I said to the ghillie, whose response I loved: 'If they weren't, something would be wrong.'

Back in the 1920s, two years after Ballantine's monster, another female angler wrote herself into the record books when Clementina Morison landed the largest ever British salmon caught on the fly, at sixty-one pounds a fish so heavy that it had to be carried from the bank of the River Deveron by horse and cart. It might have been heavier still had it been weighed on the day of capture, before water loss.

Morison went by the nickname 'Tiny', and Ballantine stood at only five foot tall. These two diminutive women had, within two years, set records that, with today's much depleted salmon population (the fish being smaller as well as fewer in number), will likely never be broken. Yet female anglers are still sometimes treated as second class, our capabilities doubted and achievements diminished. The old saying that women have a better chance of catching salmon because the fish are attracted by their pheromones is still regularly invoked, and sometimes even the women in my classes ask me if it is true.

Seeing that I was one of relatively few women only made me more determined that I would make it in this industry. Every raised eyebrow I encountered simply fed the competitive fire in me, the desire to prove not only that I could make it as a fishing professional, but that I would. I wanted it all: to fish as many rivers and go to as many places as I could; to learn more, to teach, and to inspire in others the same love as I have for angling. I wanted more people, women especially, to experience the power of fishing: the intoxicating mixture of serenity and excitement that comes with being by the water, casting a line, and the soaring feeling of achievement when a fish takes your fly.

'It's not been easy.'

My friend Jo gave the river a pensive glance as she told me the last thing I wanted to hear. I was on my first fishing trip for work, as a host – effectively a tour organiser and group leader, working with the guides, local experts who know the river and help guests to fish it. I was desperate for the trip to be a success, but Jo was telling me that the fish had not been playing ball. It made it harder to enjoy the extraordinary landscape that stretched out in front of us, but I knew that Jo and the guides were doing everything they could to make the trip a success. I was determined to make the most of the situation and learn as much as I could about fishing this new river.

We were looking out over the widest river I had ever seen, Norway's Reisa, which seemed to stretch out for ever, its cavernous breadth screened by tree-lined mountains. An epic of fjords, gorges and waterfalls, the largest of which reaches more than five times higher than the Niagara Falls, the Reisa tears down through the Arctic landscape, patrolled by eagles, snowy owls, lynx and wolves. What feels vast from the ground shrinks to a fracture in the wilderness when seen from the air. It is often likened to a natural feature carved from the mountain plateau with the blade of an axe.

This monster of a river is home to suitably massive salmon, which can exceed twenty kilos, several times larger than those typically fished in UK waters. But their size does not make them any less elusive. My friends Jo and Jonny, who ran the lodge where my fishing group was staying, admitted that not many of these giants had emerged from the massive river in the preceding days. This was their stomping ground, and no one knew better than them how good our chances over the next week would be: they could predict the success or failure of the trip. I took a deep breath, reminding myself that Norway

River Reisa, Norway.

is a notoriously difficult salmon destination, somewhere you go to catch the biggest fish but not necessarily large numbers of them.

I told myself that this would be a good day, trying to awake the inner optimist that has to be at least one half of every angler's mental make-up. Anyone who fishes regularly will have experienced the battle between hope and pessimism that we bring with us to the water. There are days when you wake up certain that the river will be fishy and you will see a salmon in your net, and others when everything feels sluggish and nothing less likely than a bite on the line.

As I surveyed the Reisa, I was trying to summon a dose of that optimism to drown out my nerves as a first-time host. In my logical mind I knew that if we didn't catch any of these salmon, it wouldn't necessarily reflect on me. If catching a trout is down to 80 per cent skill and 20 per cent chance, then the odds are reversed with salmon. The mature salmon, fully nourished from its ocean voyage, doesn't need to feed in the rivers where we fish for it. There is none of the nuance of fishing for trout, trying to match the hatch and replicate its feeding patterns, hoping to lure it onto your hook with the promise of its next meal. Often the salmon will be resting from their long and arduous migration, lying in deep pools with no motivation other than to prepare for the final leg of the journey upstream. Even after centuries in which the salmon has been sought and studied as one of angling's great prizes, the question of why it sometimes rises to take the fly remains unanswered. Much more often, the salmon simply remains unmoved.

This is little comfort to the tour leader, to whom all eyes will turn if nets remain empty for long, believing that there must be a technical answer to the reluctance of the salmon, a puzzle that knowledge or skill will solve. In my early forays as a host, I was already learning that the words, 'You're a professional, right?' came in several varieties: as query, loaded question, and occasionally tinged with accusation.

The river seemed to grow bigger and more forbidding with every glance: so much water, so many places for even these huge fish to hide away. The only cure for this anxiety, I knew, was to stop thinking and start casting. The guide had taken our group out on the boat upriver, so for the moment Jo and I were alone.

Soon I was lulled into the gentle embrace of the Spey cast with a double-handed rod. When I am fishing for salmon, I remind myself that this rhythm is an end in itself, a goal just as important as what you bring into your net. The angler cannot compel the salmon, but they can master themselves: the actions of wrist, arm and shoulder that will produce the perfect Spey cast. You watch the loops, repeat the movements and allow yourself to be subsumed by the flow of the activity. Cast, wait, take two steps downriver and cast again. The feeling of having timed this cast right, so that the current accepts your fly and sweeps it down the pool, is one of my favourites in fishing. There is something supremely relaxing about swinging out your fly and just letting the river take it, angler and water becoming one. Lulled into relaxation by the repetition, you can't help but be present in the moment, more aware of your surroundings and of the movements of your body. And often, the moment comes when you are thinking so much about the cast that you have almost forgotten that you are here to catch a fish.

A tug on the black and red sunray fly I was fishing with dragged me from my reverie. A salmon pull feels different. When fishing for trout I am hyped up and on edge, knowing that I must react straight away when it takes the fly, setting the hook before it can get away. Today I was relaxed, lulled by the calming motion of the cast, telling myself to let the fish do the work, to give it time, to be patient and not to lift the rod before the moment was right. If the cast is the most technical part of salmon fishing, and the unpredictability of the salmon the most frustrating, this — forcing yourself to wait — is the hardest. Never has patience felt more agonising than when you are a few movements away from the prize of netting a wild salmon. To rush is to risk everything.

Wait.

Only a few seconds, but they dragged endlessly, enough time to think that losing a salmon on the fly would be so much worse than never hooking into one at all. My shoulder strained, urging the familiar lifting motion. But a salmon is not a trout. It is less likely to close its mouth and bite down hard on the fly. The hook had drifted into its mouth but not yet lodged.

Wait.

In the excitement of feeling a salmon finally bite, it is all too easy to rush things, snapping at the chance like a trout to the mayfly. With a salmon on the line, this can be fatal. Lifting a hook that has not yet found the scissors – a point of purchase – risks seeing it come free. Instead the key is to pause just long enough for the fish to start doing the work for you.

Wait.

There it was, the second tug as the salmon turned its head and began to draw line from the reel.

'God save the Queen.'

I muttered the traditional words, the ones that force you to wait an extra second or two, the line slipping from your hand, before acting. This is the desperate but delicious moment between take and strike, giving the fish enough time to turn, set the hook and feel the line tighten. Then finally, with the line tightening in triumph, I could lift my rod up to the sky. I had a salmon on the hook, ready to be brought in.

I was primed for a fight, to see the salmon bucking and leaping over this vast river, and was surprised instead to feel it surrender almost meekly, with no rapid run across this wide water, no need for the dance of paying out and reeling in line until the fish was ready to come in. My friend Jo helped me to complete the catch with her net and we both peered down, admiring the beautiful fish that the river had brought us.

The distinctive purple and gunmetal colouring of this salmon, halfway between ocean silver and the pinkish hue of the mature spawner, told me that she had recently returned to the Reisa, she was just beginning to pink up but hadn't yet entirely shed the camouflage that had protected her at sea. The other notable feature was the jagged gill plate, and a long scar that ran almost the entire way down her lateral line. It was clear that this salmon had endured a fierce battle to make it home and that it had been a close-run thing: escaping a net of some sort, and presumably the sharp attention of a predator. Her body told the story of what a perilous and remarkable journey it had been, to sea and back again, through jeopardy in all its many forms.

Part of the Atlantic salmon's timeless appeal is just how much it dances with death and how many and what daunting obstacles it faces in the natural course of its life. Yet the odds, already stacked against it, are now as a result of human interference and environmental change becoming precipitously steep. The interwoven patterns of genetics and ecology that support the Atlantic salmon are being unravelled, some slowly and others with startling speed. We can see this in the sobering decline in numbers of the species recorded in its Scottish heartland.

The 35,693 Atlantic salmon caught by anglers in Scotland during the 2021 season was the lowest number on the official record, which stretches back to 1952. Almost all of these – 95 per cent in total and 99 per cent of the spring catch – were subject to catch and release. The total number represents only around three-quarters of the average catch during the previous five years, and a marked decline from 2010, when 111,400 salmon were caught in an unusually abundant season. Go back further and the trend of diminishing numbers becomes soberingly apparent. The Missing Salmon Alliance, a group of conservation organisations based in the UK, estimates that the population of mature spawners returning from the ocean has declined by at least 54 per cent and grilse by at least 40 per cent since the 1970s. Further, the Alliance believes that there has been a three- or four-fold decline in the total number of salmon swimming in the Atlantic since the mid-1980s. In Norway, the population of returning spawners is now half what it was forty years ago.

That is a tragedy not just for those who love and prize the king of fish, but for all of us. The itinerant nature of the Atlantic salmon means it sees a huge amount of the natural world during its migration and depends upon numerous habitats along the way. It is what has been called an indicator species: one of nature's early-warning systems, illustrating the health of the range of ecosystems through which it passes. The wild salmon depends on clean, fast-flowing, well-oxygenated fresh water to support its early growth and breeding; it relies upon finding sufficient food in the ocean to follow its prodigious growth curve and reach sexual maturity. And it can only survive and return home to breed when not faced with a disproportionate volume and variety of predators, themselves displaced from their natural environments, or man-made barriers such as dams and weirs that threaten to make an already difficult journey impossible.

Salmon not thriving indicates that our rivers and oceans are reaching a critical point: humanity is turning them into increasingly precarious habitats for the creatures that call them home. When one of the most resilient species on the planet is suffering, it is a reminder that none of us are protected from the consequences of our heating, increasingly hostile planet.

As I looked at the salmon in Jo's net, I was reminded of how far this fish had come to reach this point, the long miles of swimming and the multitude of dangers it had endured to return to its home river. The probability of us both arriving in this spot, at the moment I made my cast, must have been infinitesimally small. Yet chance had piled upon chance: the improbability of survival, of overcoming obstacles, and the luck of salmon fishing itself. Two journeys converged on one spot of clear Norwegian water, in one of those strangely intimate moments of connection that angling can create, as you pause to consider everything that brought you to this point and everything that propelled the fish in your net.

But those fates do not collide for long: once the salmon has rested in the net, it must be returned to the water, to continue its journey back into the invisibility from which it came. The salmon was nearing the end of her voyage; by contrast, having finally found my path, I was only just setting out on a long and uncertain journey of my own.

Chapter 5

Kiritimati, a Pacific Ocean atoll.

'Chuck the fly, *chuck the fly.*'
    My guide Kurt was shouting at me to cast as, knee deep in the turquoise water of the Indian Ocean, I struggled to get my line untangled, not having expected the moment to arrive so soon. Only moments earlier I had been asking Kurt where we would be most likely to see a giant trevally, the fish I had come to catch. Then I turned round and saw its dead eyes staring right at me, squashed surfboard of a torso halfway out of the water, drawn from the deep of the ocean to the milky flats by the sand our boots had been kicking up. All day we had thought we were hunting the GT when in fact it had been stalking us. I took in how dark its eyes were, boring into me, set within a body the colour of heavy industry – more concrete grey than silver.

It can only have been seconds, but it was enough time for the surprise to register, to take in the first glimpse of a fish I had been thinking about for weeks. Enough time for the opportunity to slip away as the gigantic fish took off, at a speed that belied its size, its flat body born to cut through the ocean with rapid intent. By the time my rod and fly were ready to cast, it was well beyond reach, and it was soon out of sight. This was my first encounter with the 'gangster of the flats', a fish with all the muscular intensity of a hundred-metre sprinter. By now I was in no doubt that I would have to be just as agile to catch one.

In search of the GT, I had come to Kiritimati, a suitably distant location for an experience that can feel like being transported into another world. Thousands of kilometres south of Hawaii and to the north-east of New Zealand, Kiritimati is one of the most isolated places on Earth, nestled by the International Date Line, effectively making it the first place in the world to welcome each new day. Travelling there is a marathon of long-haul flights and stopovers. Several people had advised me not to go, saying that if I had my heart set on a GT I would probably be wasting my time. The island was overfished, they said, and the local industry was guilty of 'chumming' (throwing bait into the water to attract fish, a practice disdained by fly fishermen).

But I was determined, and buoyed further by the fact that I would not be going alone. This big trip into the unknown was also a stepping stone for another new development in my life: my relationship with a man who immediately seemed different from all those I had previously dated – calm, supportive and the perfect person to share my fishing adventures with. B was the more experienced saltwater angler and we had already been twice to Belize to fish for permit and tarpon. With every trip

I felt more certain that this was the relationship I had spent so much time looking for.

B's presence by my side amplified an already thrilling experience: wading into the sea to fish and becoming part of the aquatic expanse, connected to the changing tones and temperatures of the water, able to see and feel where shallow flats drop off into deeper sea, capable of hunting as the predators themselves do. Even without casting a line, I loved observing the vast and unerring logic of the ecosystem, how the small fish would sometimes 'ball' into schools for protection and at other points scatter for cover; how the tropical birds would be resting on the water and then suddenly take to the air to hunt, bearing their long tails behind them like spears.

Despite the wild nature of the setting and the fish themselves, this was a cautious pursuit. Kurt had warned us to be careful not to spook these fish that can look monstrous but which are easily scared into flight, especially by the slapping of waves against the hull of a fishing boat. I had just learned the hard way that stealth must be matched by speed, when I hesitated over the GT that then suddenly shot away in a frenzy of shouts and splashes. In saltwater fishing the opportunity can arrive without warning, and it will be gone almost as quickly. You must be ready to cast every single minute. I resolved not to let my guard down again.

I would have to wait, possibly hours or days, for another window. As I anticipated the rematch there was plenty of time to seek out this ocean's other residents, taking our fill of the milkfish that travel around in huge schools, rising to the surface with their mouths open to feed on algae and small crustaceans, and the 'grey ghost' that is bonefish, their silvery flanks and moss-coloured backs blending into the cloudy waters of the flats. These ghosts are easily scared and need to be stalked, looking for the hint of a dark tail emerging from pale water as the fish presses its head against the floor to trap prey. Catching them requires a fast, accurate cast several feet in front of the nose, avoiding telltale splashes that will unnerve the fish and send it scuttling off-course. If you miss your cast and the fly falls behind the fast-moving fish, forget about trying to catch up. The bonefish is too quick, and the sensation of being chased will send it off at top speed.

Over several days on the water, wading through the flats or pursuing schools of milkfish on the boat, we had accustomed ourselves to both the challenge and the thrill of saltwater fishing. It is one thing to know that an accurate cast is required, quite another to achieve it when the wind is blowing, the water pulsing, and the fish you seek being buffeted in seemingly every direction at once. Even when you have overcome all that and got a fish on the hook, you must still contend with the awesome power of these creatures, evolved to survive in a volatile environment and more than a match for the anglers that pursue them. On one of our morning outings, B snapped a rod right in half while playing a milkfish. And that was just the warm-up act. The real monster, the GT, still lay in wait in deeper waters.

The GT was a different beast that required different tactics. Kurt advised me that my best chance was to wade out towards the deep water and start blind casting into the blue. It felt almost futile throwing the fly time after time into nothingness, a tiny lure propelled into the endless expanse of blue. Because I was not sight-fishing, the feeling of a tug on the line was a shock, electrical currents up the fingers and arm before my brain could register that this was it, a second chance. Almost as quickly came the realisation that I had not hooked into a fish but a freight train. I knew what it meant for a fish to run, sprinting and thrashing to try to free itself from the angler's hook. But the GT's flight was like nothing I had experienced before. Suddenly every warning I had read about this fish made sense: each of its yanking movements felt like it would tear the rod straight out of my hands, while its relentless retreat made me think it might pull the line and backing fully out of the reel. This was the first run: the strongest, the one that really tests whether you have tied your fly properly and brought a heavy enough rod. The guide and my boyfriend were shouting at me, but I registered nothing. My entire world had narrowed to the pursuit of something I could feel but not see. I could only cling desperately to the rod, staying in the battle by my fingertips.

This was the pure confrontation that defines saltwater fishing. Two opposing forces in a relentless tug of war. The GT pulling towards the deep ocean while I stood in the last reaches of shallows, trying to hold my position and drag it back. A minute had passed and, even using all my strength to stay upright, I began to feel almost calm. I had not lost my rod, the GT had not succeeded in pulling out my line or breaking it over the coral reefs he was swimming through. I realised I was in control. Having failed to free itself with its first burst of speed and power, each of the GT's subsequent runs became a little shorter, a shade slower. He was tiring and I was becoming more confident. I was able to hear and act on the shouted advice that I needed to pump the rod up then reel down in repeated motions, to push my rod left when the fish pulled right and vice versa, applying pressure to sap the gangster's dwindling strength.

I was playing the fish rather than fighting it, knowing that I was on the verge of letting go. Finally he came in, and there I had what every angler who wades these waters is seeking: the massive bulk of a giant trevally held in both my hands, an encounter with one of the most fearsome creatures that stalks the ocean. Its big, empty eyes gazed at me as it gave a series of grunts: *Uh, uh*. The GT is not usually the world's most aesthetically pleasing fish: moodily grey, with tar-black eyes and a gaping maw of a mouth. But mine was beautiful, with a hint of green over its back and the edges of its fins. Its scales were so smooth that I couldn't even feel them, a contrast to the raised, almost serrated edge that ran down from the lower half of the midsection to the tail, sharp enough to cut flesh — its 'lateral line', a part of the fish's sensory system that is covered in rough scales known as scutes. I clung to every moment while it rested in the water to regather its formidable strength. Then I removed the hook from its mouth and it was gone, speeding away as if nothing had happened, back to the invisibility of the deep water.

The scales of a salmon, intricate circles that combine into something halfway between a coat of armour and a camouflage system, hold the key to one of its great mysteries: where its migratory journey takes it once it has left the river to begin the ocean leg of its voyage.

The salmon's unpredictable behaviour has hampered attempts to chart its seaward journey in detail, but its scales help to reveal that story. Salmon scales are not shed and replaced but grow with the fish, adapting to new conditions and responding to what is happening in its body. Under the microscope they have patterns resembling the tightly packed circles of a fingerprint, and they contain just as much identifying information: the age of the salmon, how quickly it grew, and at what age it likely migrated from its home river. Where the 'rings' of a scale are further apart, it meant the salmon was growing faster at that point in its life.

That information allows scientists to build a picture of that salmon's life and its migratory journey. In the ocean everything is connected – the temperature of the water influences the amount of carbon that dissolves in it and the kind of plankton available for the salmon to feed upon. So the scales tell us about the water the salmon may have swum through and the food it likely consumed.

Salmon voyages are not consistent. Fish departing the same river may undertake markedly different journeys from one year to the next, while those from separate sources sometimes converge on the same distinct routes. A salmon might head north along the Norwegian coast or pursue a path to Greenland, more than 2,000 kilometres west. These choices can result in the salmon experiencing vastly different water temperature, food options and exposure to predators.

The question that defines a salmon's existence is, will it make it back to the river to spawn? The direction of its migration can determine whether it will spend one year out at sea or several; to what size it will grow; and how likely it is to encounter hostile conditions. As a creature of single-minded determination, the salmon is also in the grip of forces far beyond its control.

'How are you two *still* talking about fishing?'

The words were barely audible over the thump of the music, and the smiling shake of the head from a baffled friend said it all. I had no interest in dancing and was barely drinking. Huddled in a corner of the club, I wanted only to talk to the man with whom I had now been chatting for hours, about the one subject both of us wanted to talk about.

The conversation had started in the early evening, at the birthday party of a mutual friend. Now it was night, how late I didn't know. Everyone else had drifted to the dance floor but B and I remained in our seats, just talking, in the way that fishing people do once you realise you have found a kindred spirit who can spend the whole day, or night, comparing rivers you have fished, the flies that have been working for you that season and the equipment you have had your eye on. For most of my friends, almost nothing could be less interesting than hearing me go on about the trout I had lost or the next fishing trip I was planning. And while I had met interesting people through fishing, it was a relief to find someone I could talk to who shared my passion, without worrying that I was saying too much.

I also knew I had stumbled into something beyond the common ground of a shared hobby. This conversation that felt like it would never end had in fact been waiting to happen for more than a year. I'd first been introduced to B by his cousin, a friend who I sometimes went fishing with.

'You're the female version of him, basically,' he said to me after one day's fishing. We first met at the Game Fair, but by the time B got in touch to ask me out I was already seeing someone else. A year passed before we ended up at the same party. There the talking started, and it didn't stop until the early hours, when I took a taxi home. We had been oblivious to everyone else in the room, finding over and over again that we had not run out of things to say.

Soon we were dating, which also meant that we were fishing: weekends in Devon on the Lyd and Lew and in Hampshire on the Test. As anglers we felt like equal and opposite halves: he was a trout and saltwater fisherman who knew seemingly every beat on the Test and could show me the chalky pockets and hidden dips where the fish lie up, as well as introducing me to the world of ocean fishing. But he had never got into salmon fishing, so I could take him to Scotland to introduce him to the meditative joys of Spey casting, and the curious satisfaction of pursuing fish whose motivations and behaviour, unlike those of the trout, can never really be predicted.

B was more than just the fishing companion I had subconsciously been searching for. He also represented security and calm, things I had too often felt lacking from my life. With his large family at home up north, and a circle of friends in London, who had mostly been to university together and then moved into house-shares with each other, his was the steady, deep-rooted exist-ence that seemed to have eluded me.

My insecurity had been deepened by recent lacklustre relationships: none nearly as bad as what I had experienced in New Zealand, but still a strange succession of men who all seemed to play hard to get while we were together, but then started pressing flowers and gifts on me once we had broken up. One never let me choose the times we met, and asked me not to post photos of us together on social media (red flags!). Another, a fellow angler, berated me when I texted him about a fishing competition I had entered: how could I have not informed him before the deadline so he could also apply? It never seemed to take long to realise that somehow, yet again, I had ended up dating the wrong man.

B was different. He made no secret of the fact that he wanted a relationship with me. It was the first relationship that felt straightforward, in which I could just exist, without those agonising hours of waiting for the next message to arrive. There was so much common ground: we were both from rural upbringings in which fishing and the outdoors had played an important role; we were both in London but with a mind to leaving it before long. I could be myself around him. I knew it was serious because of my reluctance to tell any of my friends and family about him, as if sharing the news might break the spell.

Meeting B felt like the final piece in a puzzle that was finally beginning to make sense. My embryonic fishing career had come far enough for me to start considering

how I might make a living from it: I had scraps of professional experience, the backing of a sponsor, and a growing profile on social media. And my need to leave the
city felt stronger than ever. Every weekend B and I spent
out of town only confirmed the cleansing effect of the
countryside on me – the lift I would feel when I saw
fields first thing in the morning and knew that I would
be spending a good part of my day near water. For the
first year or so of our relationship, we bounced around: a
busy social life in the city, and quiet getaways to the
country whenever we could. But as we became more
serious, the pull kept getting stronger. Soon we were
talking about what a move might really entail.

The longer I lived in London and worked in my office
job, the more I had come to realise how hemmed in I
felt by the crowds and the noises, car engines drowning
out birdsong, my morning commute feeling like an
ordeal for which I would rise from my bed a little more
reluctantly each morning. I had never been a city person,
and by now knew that I would not grow into one: when
my London-loving friends talked about the things they
found reassuring – the chuntering of the trains late at
night, the snatches of boozy conversation through your
open bedroom window – I realised that these were the
exact things that interrupted the peace I craved.

When I first saw the house in Yorkshire, I knew that
we had found it. Down a gravel path, near a village but
not actually in it, surrounded by fields on all sides, near

B's family. It was the first place we saw and the only one we needed to. From the back garden I could watch the occasional steam train pass by on the adjacent railway line – a soothing sight and sound compared to the city trains. A path wended around the fields, past blackthorn bushes whose sloe berries I would pick on my autumn walks to make our own gin. A short drive took us to the River Ure, where we could join a fishing syndicate (a group of anglers who pool resources to rent regular access to a beat).

Only one thing was missing: a dog by my side. This was the other reason that I had found life in London increasingly difficult; none of my rented flats had allowed me to keep a dog and, for someone who had grown up with constant canine companionship, it was almost a form of torture to be in streets and parks in which every-one but me seemed to be walking a dog.

Recently a friend had introduced me to the rescue she had brought back from a holiday in Cyprus and let me take her out fishing for the day. It was freezing and I remember wrapping the dog up in the spare coat I had brought, her little ginger face peeking out from the swaddling. She never took her eyes off the water. I was quickly fixated on adopting a rescue of my own.

Trawling the internet for rescues, I found Wes, who would become Sedge: a bundle of fox-red fur from Romania, his chest crested with white and paw dipped in paint, a mixed breed whom I later discovered was a combination of dachshund, Pekinese, Pomeranian, shih tzu and vizsla. Without a second thought I put down the deposit for him, only later telling a bemused B, who tended towards the view that if it wasn't a pedigree Labrador then it wasn't a dog at all.

I didn't actually meet Sedge until I was driving up to Yorkshire, my entire life packed into the boot. Because I wasn't able to keep him in London, I had arranged for him to be temporarily placed with a foster family in Nottinghamshire, and I stopped by on the way to pick him up. As soon as he saw me he barked a greeting, and happily hopped into the car to assume a perch that would become familiar. As I was to learn on our first fishing trip together, when he leapt straight into the water and had to be dragged out by my ghillie, a tendency to dive in feet-first was something we had in common.

With Sedge by my side, everything changed: I moved house, moved in with my partner and launched a new career. In one sense it was impulsive and risky. After just two years of being with B, I was leaving my friends behind and starting a job with no real business plan, few relevant qualifications and scant experience as a fishing guide and coach; the work I was now hoping to make a living from. It was the same mixture of impatience, impulsiveness, determination and confidence that had led me down the bank of the Spey all those years earlier to pick up a fishing rod and starting casting unassisted because I could not bear to wait a minute longer.

But I couldn't have been happier about it. The sheer joy of having so much I wanted in front of me over-whelmed any sense of trepidation. I felt not just the excitement and anticipation of the new, but something deeper, as though I was playing the first chords of an old song that I already knew. Not for a second did I doubt that I was doing the right thing.

Chapter 6

River Ure, Yorkshire.

Our garden in Yorkshire was small, just a stone patio leading down steps to a patch of grass in front of the railway track, but it was big enough for my purposes. We did little gardening in there and planted no flowers. What I did, every morning through our first winter living there, was go outside and pick up my fishing rod; the space was just sufficient to allow me to complete the back-and-forward motions of an overhead cast.

This was not me pining for the next fishing season or hoping that the familiar rhythm of the cast could tide me through the bitterly cold winter. I had a deadline: one that I knew would do much to determine the success or failure of my embryonic fishing career. After making the move north at the turn of the year, one of the first things I had done, while we were still unpacking boxes, was to schedule my casting instructor exam for the end of March.

'If you're really serious about being an instructor, then you need to do the exam,' one of my fishing mentors, Sekhar Bahadur, had told me a year earlier. I had come to realise that he was right. I was reaching the point where you know enough to understand, as a beginner never could, how much I didn't know. I was an angler, more than capable of getting my line onto the water to make a catch. Now I needed to become a caster, in full control of fly and line, understanding without thinking which twist of the rod, tug of the line or shake of the wrist was needed depending on whether the current was fast or gentle, the wind stiff or slack, the fish rising or still.

There was only one way to do it: the Fly Fishers International casting instructor exam. The exam is a trial of twenty-two consecutive tasks that require you to demonstrate casts of different styles, speeds and distances, exhibit perfect technique, and then show that you can teach these skills to a novice. Two errors – a target missed here or a loop cast too widely there – results in immediate failure. Reading the syllabus was enough to confirm that this would be the hardest thing I had ever done: two hours in which my fly line would become a tightrope from which I could fall at any moment.

I had committed to doing all this within a handful of months. Come springtime the fishing season would begin, and I wanted to be ready, using the qualification to launch my full-time career in fishing. I was pushing myself as fast as possible, and another mentor, Chris Hague, gently warned me that he would not allow me to go forward for the test unless he was confident that I could pass. 'You'll never be at your best on the day,' he said. 'Or you'll have rain and high winds. So you have to be at 110 per cent going in.'

Catch

The only answer was to go outside each and every morning with my fishing rod and measuring tape. Down on the grass went three targets, and I began the ritual: a cast to twenty feet, the fly dropping inside the first hula hoop. Then several false casts, backward and forward to get the fly airborne again, releasing more line from my hand as I did so, no markings to guide me, just the knowledge earned through repetition that *this* much was enough to get me to thirty feet with the second cast, and forty-five with the third. Then all three, again and again, dropping the fly into each target until the motions of the cast and the rhythm of paying out more line became things I couldn't fail to do. Until I was certain that I was doing all this without letting my loops exceed the mandated four-foot-wide limit, or straying from a straight line as I lifted and accelerated my rod tip back and forward, or letting the fly touch the ground – *the floor is water* – between casts. Only the percussive chanting of the steam train, speeding behind me on schedule at the bottom of the garden, reminded me that time was passing.

Distance work done, I turned to roll casts, which are the basis of a Spey, making sure my D-loop was not billowing beyond the length of my rod and arm combined. I taught myself the techniques required to manipulate how the line moves across the water, introducing slack to limit the effect of drag (so preventing the fly from moving at an unnaturally quick pace). This

145

involved the wiggle mend: a shaking of the wrist after the forward cast is completed to send calming wave patterns through your fishing line. I practised big wiggles and small ones, short casts and long ones, checking and double-checking that I had not made any disqualifying technical error. With Chris, who I met every fortnight for a coaching session, I would go to the local football field, where we would use the touchline to ensure that I was lifting the rod tip through a perfect 180-degree plane – the first of the five essentials of fly casting. Back at home, I narrated my efforts to the horses grazing in the adjacent field, the closest thing I had to an available student to teach.

The routine became monotonous because monotony was the point: drilling myself with constant repetition, until there could be no doubt, no hesitation about how much line I needed or how much power a certain distance required. I would wake up feeling the stiffness in my shoulders and begin casting, often on days so cold that I could hardly feel my fingers. One February morning I went outside to find my fishing rod on the patio, where I always left it, covered in snow.

I persevered because it felt like the most important thing I had done in my life, and because I realised it was working. Occasionally B, who until now had been the more experienced and capable angler, would come out to watch me work and have a go himself, sometimes finding that he couldn't match my distance or accuracy.

'She's better than me now,' he would joke when we met up with friends.

That winter seemed to last for ever, my world shrunken to a few small patches of frozen grass as I went through the tasks again and again. By the time late March came round, Chris and I agreed that I was ready. But even as my skills improved, and the necessary movements became muscle memory, the exam loomed as a forbidding obstacle. I am generally a confident person, but I struggle with public performance. I hate the knowledge that people will be watching and judging. Rather than thinking through what I need to say and do, I become obsessed with what I will get wrong: the fear grows and grows that perhaps it would have been better not even to try. In a school production of *Grease*, I was cast as Cha-Cha. Standing in the wings in her black, floral-patterned halterneck, I was suddenly overcome with such a strong dose of stage fright that I almost had to be shoved into the scene. Even today, when I spend a good amount of my time in front of either a camera or an audience, I have to prepare carefully and remind myself that I know what I am doing.

I was feeling increasingly anxious and stressed about the casting exam. In the days leading up to it, I went to stay with my grandparents in Stratford. I sat by the fire in their cozy sitting room while my grandpa went to the cupboard, returning with a bottle of homemade sloe gin.

'This is my cure-all,' he said with a wink. 'It'll take the edge off your nerves.'

I poured myself a glass and took a sip. The gin was sweet and tart, and it burned my throat just a bit.

I took a deep breath and told my grandpa I wished I didn't have to go through with the exam, but knew it was something I could not avoid. Fail at this and my fishing career, which I had now been working towards for almost four years, would stall in the starting blocks. And it was important that I pass first time, I said. While the test could be retaken, I could not face putting myself through another spartan winter of training; nor could I really afford to lose time or income in the approaching summer season.

I told him how desperate I was to succeed, to show that I could do it, and that I belonged in this industry. That it felt like now or never. He listened patiently, nodding his head occasionally and just offering the odd word of encouragement. One shot turned into two and then three, and somehow by the time I went to bed, Grandpa and I were giggling as we walked upstairs to our bedrooms.

I left feeling lighter and more confident. I knew that I had prepared as best I could. And I knew I had the support of my family, and that was all I needed.

The day itself began with a couple of hours in the classroom for the written theory test. Then we were outside and the practical exam, the real challenge, began: I undertook the tasks, which had become grimly familiar, but this time in front of an audience of three examiners. It was a stop-start experience in which, after every exercise, the trio would make notes on their clip-boards and confer with each other. Two strikes and they would deliver the dreaded tap on the shoulder to say that there was no point continuing. I had spent months care-fully rehearsing each exercise, but nothing had prepared me for the watching and waiting in between, and the feeling of dread as each consultation seemed to take longer than the last. But somehow the thumbs-down did not come and I carried on, through wide and tailing loops, fast and slow casts, long and short distances. Into the teaching tasks, with one of the examiners acting as my student, I told myself I was back in the garden at home, talking to the horses.

Then it was over and I could only watch as the three people who held my future in their hands went into a final discussion. Years of my life and months of dedicated training had narrowed to this moment, where I could do nothing more than look at my fishing rod lying on the grass and hope. I could hear low voices but not catch any of their words. Nor did I make eye contact with the one other candidate who had made it through to this stage. Finally one of the three started to walk towards me, ambling as if the moment held no importance.

'You passed.'

He smiled, inviting one in return. But as the meaning of the words landed I found myself sobbing, hands on my knees, hardly able to stand. All the nervous energy that had gone into the day, all the doubts I had suppressed about whether I could succeed and all the hopes I had invested into changing my life to do this came out of me. I raised my head to see three concerned faces looking back at me, clipboards hugged to their chests, clearly confused about what to say or do next. I gathered myself, thanked them and made my way to a waiting B, who had been observing the whole thing from a distance. He drove us home through the pale spring sunlight. Our new life ready to begin.

'We'll start here.'

It was the start of the day and the first pool of the beat. The morning chill seemed to add a snap of anticipation as I took in the Ure, a quintessential Yorkshire river that flows over seventy miles through Wensleydale, down the falls at Aysgarth, surrounded by the limestone grasslands that help to give flavour to the famous local cheeses.

I was guiding a solo client as a newly minted fishing instructor. In one of my first jobs of the season, I was trying to give every impression that I had been doing this for years and not mere months. I stepped assertively into the calf-deep water, acting like I had found just the right spot to begin fishing. Except the water was higher than usual and my feet did not find ground. My body plunged forward, arms lost behind me as I went down, face-first in the water. Quite a look for a professional fishing guide. As I got out of the water and told my concerned client that no, I was fine, thanks, and I didn't need to change, I could feel that my clothes were soaking beneath my wading jacket. I spent the rest of the day trying not to shiver in the chilly spring air.

Another time it wasn't me who got soaked but the client. On Tanfield Lake, a picturesque spot nestled in an upper corner of the Yorkshire Dales, with the River Ure flowing close by, I was giving a client her first ever solo fishing lesson. We had waded into the lake and were starting to cast when I realised I'd left something on the bank. 'Aim towards that, I'll be back in a second,' I said, pointing to a little island in the middle of the water. Turning back a minute later, I saw her wading out towards the island. She was in so deep that she was practically swimming. My instruction had not been clear enough, especially for a novice, and she had thought I meant she should go to the island, not cast at it.

Fortunately, she was laughing as she stripped off her wet clothes to change.

Unbeknownst to us, another angler happened to approach from the ridge and stumbled upon my client in her underwear. His face immediately drained of colour, and as he walked past us he quietly remarked, 'I don't usually witness something like that while fishing.' Since then, she and I have become friends.

More wake-up calls were to come as I completed my first season as a coach. I had to learn how to teach fishing, and, crucially, I had to discover what good coaching really meant. To begin with I was too eager to please, to ensure that every student went home happy and with at least one catch to talk about and photograph. I would cut short time teaching the fundamentals of casting to ensure that my novice clients could skip to the good part. Now, with years more experience, I appreciate the wisdom that teaching a woman to fish is so much more valuable than helping her to catch one. I have the confidence to insist that we complete the casting drills on grass, and to be more didactic in telling people how to stand, hold and move the rod properly, correcting basic errors around timing and the application of power.

Back then I was more tentative, worried that the lessons wouldn't be fun, and still learning the nuances of teaching male or female clients (the women generally being more attentive listeners, the men focused more on casting as far and fast as possible), sheer novices or those who had fished before. I met all these kinds of students and more as I rushed through my first season coaching and guiding, doing as much as possible and willing to go almost anywhere in order to work. Friends and family were introducing me to people who wanted to improve their skills or just enjoy a day on the water, and I relied on word-of-mouth referrals from one client to the next.

I did some work on lakes local to where we had moved, hosted ladies', kids' and beginners' days all over the country and leaned on my early experience to host trips to Scotland. As much as I had cloistered myself at home during the winter months to prepare for the casting exam, I now went relentlessly on the road, feeling unable to turn down any offer of work, pushing myself through day after day of long drives, early starts and late nights.

By my side was Sedge, who having become used to my company now refused to relinquish it. When I packed a bag to go away, he would lie next to the suitcase; then when I was putting everything into the car he would sneak through the open door, just in case I forgot him. On those long road trips, when I would often park up at a service station to steal some sleep before the drive home, he would jump onto my chest when I put the seat back, and remain in exactly the same spot until I woke up.

Never was Sedge more himself than by the water. I have not met anyone, human or animal, who seemed to relish the sport of fishing as much as him. Having come from a Romanian kennel, he seemed to drink in every second in the open countryside, taking his fill of the sensory overload that surrounded him. From the moment I first took him to the river and he responded by immediately springing into the water, he showed an obsession with all things fishing. He would watch the water as intently as any angler, his little legs creeping right to the edge when I hooked into something, and then barking his instructions just at the point when the fish was ready to be brought in. If Sedge couldn't get a good view, he would create one. Sometimes he would know someone had a fish in their hands but be unable to see it, like when I or one of my clients was lying flat on the ground, hands in the water about to release the fish, or crouching in the river itself, a level down from the steep bank. A thud and a bark would tell you that Sedge had landed, hopping onto your back so he could peer over your shoulder, desperate to get a glimpse of that final tail kick as a trout or salmon disappeared back out of sight. Sometimes he would swim to the other side and sit looking at me, head tilted as if to say, when are you coming to get me?

I needed his support during those early days, when I was clocking up miles travelling the country more easily than I was bringing in the money to make this new career viable. Being eager to take on work, and knowing that I had to make my name, meant I often ended up doing jobs that barely covered my expenses. Between media work, sponsorships and guiding clients I was making just about enough to cover my half of our living costs, but less than I had done working in a London office, and far from a level that made it feel like a sustainable career.

'You can't do everything for free,' my mother would say, and after my frustration had subsided I came to know the truth of what she was saying. A career in fishing was proving to be everything I had hoped for: the chance to travel, to spend my days by the water, and to feel the joy of watching someone catch a fish for the first time, knowing that I had helped them to do so. I loved the challenge of teaching, adapting my methods to each student; some wanted lots of information and hands-on guidance, others a few succinct instructions and room to experiment; each one, like the fish themselves, was their own particular riddle. Yet for all of this, I knew that I hadn't yet cracked the code of how to turn something I loved into a career I could live off. I was learning the truth of why people in the fishing industry like to say that you'll never be a millionaire in this business. We all do it for love and excitement; making the money work isn't so easy.

These thoughts would sometimes twist through me on the long drives home from a day of guiding, with Sedge snoring softly on the seat next to me. But they would be set aside when I was back on the water, or when I made what felt like the next breakthrough: a new client who could potentially introduce me to several more, or an opportunity to raise my profile in the industry.

Or when I went travelling. I made trips during this period to destinations including Alaska, Sweden and Iceland. I was able to bring my mum to fish what is one of the most plentiful places for Atlantic salmon, Iceland's famously wide rivers, with their desolate settings and rocky surrounds. It was a precious occasion, harking back to the Scottish holidays that had been such an important part of our relationship as mother and daughter. But now the roles had reversed. Increasingly, she was focused single-mindedly on the catch, while I had become the guide and facilitator. I took great pleasure in being able to take the lead and help her fish, as she had for so long done for me. Our relationship had changed with the passage of time, but fishing remained its golden thread: the essential link between us, connecting past to present.

The question of how long the mature salmon will remain at sea before beginning its journey home is yet another of its life's great mysteries. There is no consistent pattern: some will return after a single winter, while others may continue feeding and growing for as long as five years before attempting to get home. This decision, conscious or otherwise, is a classic evolutionary trade-off. There are advantages to remaining longer in the ocean, where the salmon can grow to a significantly larger size (as much as twenty kilos after three winters at sea, ten or even twenty times larger than some grilse). Each year spent at sea allows the salmon to double in mass. Yet the longer it lives in the ocean, the more it remains exposed to the jeopardy that comes with swimming and feeding alongside deadly predators. The prize of a longer ocean stint may be significant in evolutionary terms, but the cost of pursuing it can also be total.

This dilemma is particularly acute for the hen (female) salmon, who generally stay for longer in the ocean's waters, needing more time to feed and support the development of their reproductive system – a task towards which they commit approximately six times more energy than male salmon. As she readies her body for the work of egg production, the hen faces another of the innately complex calculations for which only centuries of evolution can have prepared her. The larger in size she grows, the larger her eggs will be – a good portent for the survival of her offspring, who can themselves expect to be born larger, better able to compete for resources and ward off predators. A size advantage will also help her to claim and defend prime spawning grounds back in the natal river, where the water flows fastest and is most oxygenated. Yet the larger hen also produces her eggs more slowly; so there are diminishing returns on the investment of spending more time at sea for the sake of growth and future fertility. At some point the salmon makes an instinctive call: enough time has been spent among the dangers of the ocean, any more simply increases the risk of death for a negligible benefit.

We don't know exactly what combination of physiology and environment compels the hen to begin her journey back to the river where she was born and now hopes to give birth herself. Whatever the case, it is yet another example of the fine-tuned judgements the salmon must make in a journey that constantly pits the instinct for survival against the urge to push on towards completing the migration that is its life's purpose.

After moving to Yorkshire, I knew, almost everything in my and B's life would change. But the one thing I had expected to remain constant was our relationship. For two years before we moved into our house we had been close to inseparable, spending all our time together even though we lived apart, escaping the city to go fishing whenever we could, and immediately fitting in to each other's social lives.

The move north was something we had both wanted. Yet neither of us seemed entirely happy once we were living this shared dream rather than striving for it. I knew that the nature of chasing my dreams meant I was often away but, when I made suggestions for things we could do together, he increasingly rejected them. It meant that, more often than not, I would make trips down to London to see friends, go rock climbing and fish purely for leisure on my own.

Then when we did go out, a switch would flip and suddenly he didn't want to let me out of his sight. I would be off chatting with friends – our friends – and he would appear by my side, a drink in hand. There were whole days when he didn't want to know, and then nights when he became like my shadow.

But these were ripples on an otherwise still surface, hardly enough to stir real doubt as we embarked on the shared life that we had been planning for two years, and which I had been thinking about for much longer. The picture postcard that had formed in my mind when my parents separated – that I would have a happy marriage and family of my own, a beautiful house in the country, we would all love each other and it would be perfect – now seemed to be within reach. The pieces I did not already have I could imagine: the children we would have, and how I would take them down to the lake as my mother had me, the looks on their faces when they first felt the wriggle of a fish in their hands, the pop of joy and wonder that comes when you learn that the water is not just wet but alive.

Having children had long been at the forefront of my mind. I'd dreamed of having my first by twenty-five, the age I now was. So when B proposed, six months into our time in Yorkshire, I didn't hesitate in saying yes. Marriage had always been the natural next step: we wanted it, both our families expected it and no one questioned its inevitability.

Less seamless was the planning of the wedding, where, despite my natural inclination to assertiveness, I soon found myself sinking into the background. I had wanted something small, more cosy country than white wedding. Yet as we sat round our kitchen table, my family and his, our guest list and theirs, it soon became clear that I would not be able to fight the tide of other people's plans. Eager to please and unwilling to risk treading on toes, I let myself be carried along.

Rather than basking in the moment, I felt stressed: assailed by menu choices, colour palettes, table plans and set lists. I realised that, for all I had thought about getting married and having a family of my own, I had never actually daydreamed about my wedding day, the dress I would wear or the music we would have our first dance to.

Instead I retreated to fishing. Here I could not get enough of planning: the next adventure, next client, next sponsorship gig or media opportunity. Here I felt like I was making progress and had control. And when doubts pricked at me as I drove myself to a job, or drifted off for a roadside nap at the end of a long day, I told myself it was natural: that what often felt like misgivings were in fact symptoms of stress from running on the twin treadmills of my home life and my job, which never seemed to stop.

I had to keep reassuring myself like this, for stray comments that had hardly registered at the time were now starting to come back to me. Advice from a good friend's mother, years ago and long before B was on the scene. 'If you ever have any reservations about whether you should marry someone, trust them.' And more recently my father, who had taken me aside after we got engaged. 'I couldn't be happier for you. But if there's ever a time when you feel like something isn't right, remember you don't have to go through with it.'

In the difficult period that was to follow, I would often think about these words, wondering why I hadn't taken them more seriously at the time. I would think back to a conversation with my friend a few months before the wedding, when I finally gave voice to my misgivings and said I thought, perhaps, what her mother had warned about was happening to me. I recalled her sympathetic smile: one that said she understood, but wasn't it getting a bit late for this now, and did I really want to blow everything up for a case of cold feet?

In the end I was, am, someone who prefers to do things than to doubt them. I told myself again that this was what I wanted; reminded myself that B was the man I had fallen in love with.

As we left the church on our wedding day, chaperoned by an honour guard of fishing rods, on to our reception by the lake where I had first learned to fish as a child, any flickering doubts had been snuffed out by the significance and joy of the occasion. I was near the place I considered home, marrying the man I thought of as my best friend, and achieving one of my deepest ambitions for my life.

I had been thinking about this moment almost since that first night we had sat together, talking and talking about fishing, so wrapped up in the discovery of each other that we simply ignored everything around us. Our relationship had sprung from that kernel: B's trout fisherman to my salmon angler, a singular passion and a shared bond. I had always assumed that the two halves – our relationship and our careers – would twist together into an unbreakable knot, each stronger for the other's presence. I had never considered that the two might, in fact, start to pull against each other. Nor was I in any way prepared for how quickly they could unravel.

Chapter 7

Isla Holbox, Mexico.

As I held the tarpon, feeling its forked tail fluttering against my hand, dipped in the warm Mexican water, contentment settled over me. This was the culmination of two pursuits: of the 'silver king', a giant that can weigh in at over a hundred kilos, and of my search for someone with whom to share moments like this.

When B and I had told people that we were going fishing for our honeymoon, most rolled their eyes or laughed. What was romantic, they asked, about days that begin early and end late, spent sweating out on a boat, not alone in each other's company but chaperoned by guides? Did we really want to return to our beachside shack after dark each night, drenched through and smelling of fish?

Yet neither of us had ever seriously considered that we would do anything else. Fishing had begun our relationship and to a great extent it had *been* our relationship: a constant run of weekends away and trips abroad, being the couple who fished together, always pushing each other on to the next place and the next catch.

Now for this most important of trips we were in search of a special fish: the tarpon, at once acrobat and warrior, which once hooked will leap high out of the water to try to detach itself from the fly. Its elegance and athleticism has made the silver king the favoured catch of many famous anglers, including several American presidents (from FDR, who was filmed catching a 77-pound tarpon in 1937, to George Bush Sr, who was in his eighties when he landed one almost twice that size in the Florida Keys). Now B and I would begin our marriage in pursuit of the same goal.

On Isla Holbox, flamingos line the beaches and the green-tinged water of the flats cuts gentle channels through the trees. Mangroves perch up on spidery wooden roots as though straining for a better view, and the pursuit of tarpon feels almost soothing. The water is clear enough to see the fish and the wind seems to come in short gentle breaths. As our boat drifted across the water, I almost began to feel that this was a romantic holiday after all.

We were watching and waiting for something: a sighting of silver not just moving through the water but *rolling*, the rhythmic gymnastics of the tarpon rising to the surface, where it will take quick breaths of air to fill its swim bladder. This was the moment to cast, to turn the close, still heat of the morning into frenzy. I could hear our guide Alejandro, a legendary tarpon fisherman known universally as Mr Sandflea, shouting. The hitherto gentle water began to writhe as the tarpon bit and twisted. And then the sight we had come here to see, for which we had traded in honeymoon suites and couples' massages. The silver king jumped, shaking as it leapt a rainbow across the water. With my new husband by my side, the pull of the line at full stretch, and the sight of one of the ocean's greatest fish arcing through the air in front of me, I knew this was a moment I would always be able to close my eyes and recall. As I brought the tarpon in I just gazed at it; the light being thrown off the rhombus patterns of the gills, the platinum glare that protects it from predators. Even a minor spat with B, who fumbled the photo as I crouched holding the fish, could not sap the joy I felt. I was convinced that only good things lay ahead of us.

Every wedding marks both a beginning and an end. For B and me, it was the conclusion of a time in our lives when everything seemed to be changing all at once. So many things had happened, in such quick succession. The move to Yorkshire had been followed by my monastic pursuit of the casting exam, our engagement and the planning of the wedding, all while we were both trying to launch new freelance careers – me in fishing and him in field sports. There had been so much to plan and to do and so little time to talk and think, to understand who we were becoming as people, both in our late twenties and starting to work out what we really wanted from life.

Now we were married, eighteen months had passed since we moved to Yorkshire, and we had both settled into our new careers. It was only as this pace of change slowed down that I started to realise how much I had been hiding behind being busy. Until now, when B was in one of his distant moods, or when I felt myself retreating into my work, I could rationalise it away: we were both under pressure and there was so much to do. Things would settle down.

Now they had settled and we could no longer avoid the reality of where our relationship had drifted to. Somehow fishing, which had brought us together in the first place, seemed to have become both the symptom and source of a conflict that was increasingly difficult to attribute to teething problems. When the opportunity of an exciting trip came up – to Iceland in search of salmon, or the Caribbean for saltwater fishing – B was the person I immediately wanted to share it with. His was the fishing brain I wanted to pick about the challenges of a new destination, getting lost in the details of equipment and tactics. Even better, I wanted him to come with me as my partner, continuing our relationship the way it had started, fishing as the heartbeat. I had thought he wanted this too. But now every invitation I put his way was rejected. He wanted to stay at home. In my mind, our shared house in Yorkshire was the base from which we would explore the world together. I soon found that, in his, the base was all that he needed. Settling down suddenly seemed to be clipping our wings. It felt like he was closing the door on the adventurous side of our relationship just as I was pushing at it. Increasingly I was having to do alone what I had always assumed we would share together. It wasn't just travel and fishing where B seemed to be withdrawing; whenever I wanted to go down to London to see friends or we were invited to an event, it was a struggle to get him to accompany me. Sometimes he flat out refused, and on a few occasions he cancelled at the last minute, leaving me to go alone.

I knew the move had changed our relationship in ways we had not explicitly acknowledged or adjusted to. I had gone from a steady office job to one where I worked long and irregular hours; I was also investing all my spare time and energy in my fishing career. I knew B wanted more of my attention, and I wanted to give it to him; there were days when I felt guilty that I was spending another evening working, focused on my laptop and not my husband. But I also expected more of his understanding – that I was at a make-or-break stage in my career, and that I was the one who had gone further out on a limb, moving to a place where he had family and friends and I had none. I was desperate to close the gap that seemed to be growing between us. But I was also fighting – against the simple reality that there was too much to do, and perhaps even more so against my instinct to close myself off in difficult situations, to take a step away from the pain rather than trying to grasp it.

I was annoyed, too, that he often seemed ambivalent when I tried to talk about work, to share the successes and chew over the failures. One day I was invited to help host a fishing outing with several local celebrities. It felt like a move in the right direction, another indication that I could turn my passion into a sustainable way of life. But more than that, it was just an exciting opportunity. When I got home I couldn't wait to tell B about who I had met, and what it had been like rubbing shoulders with people we were used to seeing on the TV. But when I got through the door and found him on the sofa, he just looked at me blankly as I started talking. After a few seconds, without saying anything, he walked straight past me and out of the room.

Some relief came when we returned to the safer ground of fishing, when we were invited to go away with a group of friends. We went back to Mexico, this time in pursuit of permit, a flat fish that is hard to spot and even harder to catch. With its silver body, round at the front and rapidly tapering towards the tail, the permit does not appear aqua-dynamic – more like a misshapen pancake cutting its improbable path through the water. But though large and slightly ungainly, the permit is also quick-witted and aggressive. It is wary, equipped with massive eyes and a deep nasal cavity to detect danger at a distance, and possessed of a distance runner's kick when it senses trouble or has bitten onto a hook. Best sought across open water where it cannot quickly find its way to cover, the permit is one of a trio regarded as the 'grand slam' of saltwater fishing, alongside the tarpon and bonefish.

Technically you only complete the grand slam by catching all three fish within a 24-hour period. But anyone who has fished for permit will know that there are days when just seeing and casting at a fish, let alone landing it, feels like an achievement. These creatures make an extreme sport of elusiveness, helped by their bodies' natural camouflage and early-warning systems. Sometimes the glimmer of a yellow-brown fin or the flash of darkness of the deeply forked tail are the only clue that it is present in the water.

During our week-long holiday, we became familiar with the frustration that is an unavoidable, engrossing part of permit fishing. We had gone for days on the boat hardly seeing anything, and I had made perhaps five proper casts over the course of almost a week. Then, on our last day, everything changed. The permit is a schooling fish, typically moving and feeding in groups of around ten. However, larger specimens might be found alone or in smaller schools. Suddenly the water, ominously blank for days on end, was a shimmering and shuddering mass of life.

We pursued in the boat, keeping pace but also maintaining a wary distance. We knew that to get too close would send the permit running, but also that we had to be close enough for a long-distance cast to reach the school. It is a classic saltwater fishing dilemma, where reward only comes through the right balance of boldness and subterfuge, respecting the wary nature of the fish as much as its raw power.

The permit is an unforgiving adversary. There can be no mistakes when the moment comes: the fly must be correctly chosen, the rod properly set up, the cast fast and accurate, followed by smooth strips of the line help the fly to travel at the same speed as the water.

When the chance to strike presented itself, I was standing on the bow of the boat, ready to cast, and B quickly changed my fly. I felt a tingling thrill as I cast into the group and felt a large one take, tensing as I waited for the fish to set off on a galloping horse of a run. But instead of the tug, I felt a drop, my stomach lurching as if on a fairground ride, taut line suddenly going slack. As I dragged it in, a closer look confirmed that the fly had slipped off at the exact point where the knot should have been securing it. B had tied it and I looked round to see that his face was flushed; he had realised what a bad error he had made.

He knew as well as I did how precious a bite from a permit is. The fish's eyes, deep, dark wells facing out to either side, make it highly attuned to danger even by the standards of ocean dwellers. As picky eaters who feed mostly on shrimp and crab, and who take fright at the first sign of something untoward in the water, permit are known for being perhaps the hardest ocean fish to tempt onto the fly. Hooking into one is hard. Losing it is unforgivable.

But there wasn't time for frustration. The schooling permit were still within reach, but could slip away at any moment. So I said nothing about the mishap, not taking a second look behind me; my concentration on the water was total. At the next opportunity I made my cast, slowing the forward motion ever so slightly, making sure the fly dropped gently onto the water. I pulled the line back in slow, gentle strips, letting the crab fly sink below the surface. First the sneaking and then the snatch, the grab and the exhilaration of tension on the line. This time it held. I soon had my catch, and admired the dark patch graffitied onto the permit's otherwise smoothly silver flank, and its gumshoe lips, slowly opening and closing as if in surprise.

I held on to the fish, feeling the excitement spiked with exhaustion that is saltwater fishing's addictive cocktail. As I looked at B, he at me, and both of us at the permit, I knew that I wanted my life and our marriage to be made of moments like these: the battle, the achievements, the forgiveness of mistakes, the togetherness that comes through situations where there is no space for anything else. Just a fish to be watched, a fly to be tied and a cast to be made. Then on to the next place, the next adventure, the next fish to spend weeks thinking about, days in pursuit of and precious minutes where the battle between us on a distant spot of water would grow to fill our entire world.

For much of their lives to this point, the male and female salmon have had largely interchangeable existences. That changes once they have returned to the river, at which point their bodies alter again and their life expectancy begins to diverge. While some hens will survive to repeat the great adventure of migration – becoming multi-spawners, or kelts – relatively few of their male mates will. The way they ready themselves to breed leaves those that make it to the finish line drained in the aftermath, prone to predation, disease and exhaustion.

The cock salmon's requirements for mating are signified by another dramatic change in its physiology. It loses the teeth it grew for the purpose of feeding and replaces them with longer incisors that attach themselves to a jaw that can grow significantly bigger than it was before, developing into a hooked shape known as a 'kype'. Together, sharper teeth and curved jaw form what is in effect a weapon for fighting, anticipating the highly competitive nature of breeding for the male.

In parallel, its outward appearance evolves. Hormonal changes encourage the release of pigments including melanin, helping to turn the silvery colour of its body to something between brown and bronze, and carotenoid, which promotes the appearance of pinkish-red spots over its lower jaw and flanks. Both are adaptations designed to communicate vitality and virility both to potential mates and competing males.

Once matured in this way, the cock is ready to patrol likely spawning grounds, fighting with competing males either directly – using its new equipment to bite or head-butt opponents – or through forms of display that allow him to establish dominance. Typically, one alpha male in a group will accept the presence of several smaller, less viable mates, but aggressively try to repel an alpha of equivalent stature. Sites at which a hierarchy of this kind has been clearly established encourage the hen to dig her redd, whereas she may abandon a nascent nest if continued aggression between prospective suitors suggests a more ambiguous picture.

The male salmon has had to survive much to reach this point. But the return to his home river, far from signifying a place of calm and retreat from danger, actually brings him into the most intense competition of his life so far. Having spent years eluding danger, now he must adapt, growing prouder and more forceful as he pursues the end to which his life's journey has been leading him.

Hard work had allowed me to fashion a foothold in fishing, but it still felt uncertain and I knew that I could not sustain the pace of my first season as a professional, constantly on the road. It was not only exhausting but challenging professionally. Being a fishing guide without a home water is a little like being a tour guide who takes people around a different city each week.

I could have settled for securing access to some beats on the Ure and trying to bring the clients to me. But I wanted something more, the chance not just to teach fishing but to share my love for the sport and inspire something of the same in as many people as possible. Ever since I had started doing lunchtime sessions teaching casting in Green Park, I had nurtured a thought that I had hardly mentioned to anyone: the idea of creating my own fishing school. The one thing I loved almost as much as fishing itself was showing others how to do it, especially beginners. I pictured a future in which I would spend the domestic season running the school and the winter months travelling the world, one dream destination at a time.

The school would be my business, but it was also a personal mission. I knew I was still not entirely accepted in the fishing world. Whatever I did, disobliging comments and questions would soon appear underneath my Instagram posts or be reported back to me via others. When I appeared in a newspaper article, I was putting it on for the camera. When I posted on Instagram, I was a clothes horse who couldn't really cast. Even when I became a certified casting instructor, it was only – these faceless critics claimed – because I was a woman with a growing media profile, and the casting instructors had done me a favour. I was constantly reminded that some people would always resent my presence in fishing simply because I was young, blond and female.

Part of this was the soft misogyny that most women who fish (or do just about anything) have experienced: the raised eyebrows when you make a catch, comments about your clothing, questions about whether 'she' can really cast. And some of it was more targeted: an almost vitriolic response to my profile on social media and the way I promoted my fishing work, with negative comments about everything from my technique to the times when I painted my nails with a pattern of trout scales.

At points this has become more serious; stalkers have targeted me on several occasions. By far the worst was a year-long campaign by two people who harassed me, my mother, friends and sponsors. As well as the abusive and derogatory comments on social media, they made it plain that their intent was to tear me down and destroy my career. Initially I tried to ignore it, having already learned that responding to critical comments simply encouraged more. But it was so hateful, and went on for so long, that it was impossible not to be affected. Every time I blocked a profile another one would spring up with the same messages, same tone of voice, same relentless daily pattern. It got to the point where I would wake up in the morning knowing that the first thing I would read was a message from them. And of course I worried that they might try to find me in the real world. But worst of all was the feeling of insecurity that comes with being a target, and realising that being in the public realm makes you fair game in the eyes of a tiny minority who will impose the frustrations and inadequacies of their own lives onto yours. I was wondering whether to escalate the situation when suddenly the abuse stopped. They finally either got bored or moved on to their next target. It has happened again since, but never to the same extent. I still sometimes think about the fact that one of the trolls was father to a daughter.

My response to social media abuse would change from one day to the next. Sometimes it really got me down. It is hard not to be affected at the end of a long day when someone gets in touch to call you a fraud who knows nothing about fishing. And a constant reminder that there are people in the world who don't like you is more demoralising than it should be.

But mostly I tried to brush it aside, remind myself that it was irrelevant, and use it as fuel to the fire of my ambition. Although I knew that many of these voices would never be silenced whatever I did and how I did it, I also wanted to prove them wrong. Setting up a school would be my way of doing that: furthering my career and answering my critics at the same time.

For all that motivation, however, I was short on practicalities. Alongside the big idea was an almost complete lack of knowledge about how to implement it. There was no business plan, no timeline, no strategic vision: just a thing I wanted to achieve and a sense that I could will it into being.

Undaunted, I started casting around on Google Maps for lakes in the local area that I might be able to persuade the owner to let me use for fishing lessons. After a few false starts I had my breakthrough, in a place I would never have foreseen. In fact, when I approached the Swinton Estate, home to a hotel, country club and 20,000 acres of land, I did not even mention my idea for a fishing school. I thought there was no chance that such a prestigious venue would take a punt on a speculative idea being put forward by someone with almost no experience. Having fished Swinton's tree-shrouded beats on the Rivers Ure and Burn the previous season, I enquired about hosting some corporate days there, mirroring the work I was already doing on the Test.

This was what I expected to discuss when the owner and hotel manager agreed to meet me. Then a stray remark, one I will always remember, caught me by surprise and changed everything.

'So, what's your plan?'

Before I could stop myself I was pouring it all out: how my love for fishing was only matched by my passion for teaching others to love it too; the vision for a school, the lake that reminded me of where I had first fished for trout, my fondness for the country setting and the barn buildings. I was pitching the idea I had had no intention of proposing, to people whom I never would have imagined would be open to it.

It sounded like a good idea, they said. Where was I planning to base it? When I admitted that an idea was all it currently was, I was stunned by their immediate, almost casual response. Swinton had a few lakes and could easily give one over to a project like this. There was plenty of indoor space. A school sounded like a good way of introducing more people to the Estate and offering something new to hotel guests. By the end of the meeting I had come away with something I never would have thought possible: a commitment to work together to establish my fishing school at Swinton.

It was a better base than I had dared to hope for, the lakes adjacent to a deer park and the estate itself a rolling wonder of the Yorkshire countryside, encompassing forest, grouse moor and parkland. Its centrepiece is Swinton Park, a Georgian country house that was converted into a castle with Gothic features at the beginning of the nineteenth century and which now functions as a hotel. There could be nowhere better for people looking to escape the rush of urban life and start to attune themselves to the quiet rhythms of the countryside.

There was no opportunity to bask in the moment, however. Our meeting was in late January, just a few months before the fishing season would begin in earnest. Neither Swinton nor I saw any reason to lose a year, so we forged ahead, determined that the school would be up and running in time to welcome guests that season. It felt like an hourglass had been turned over. Every day that passed, the sand seemed to be rushing faster to the bottom as I scrambled to get everything in place for the launch. And every day I discovered something new I hadn't thought of or realised we would need.

It was a task with endless requirements. There was the site itself – permits and insurance to be secured, a lake to be stocked, the indoor space to be refurbished into a miniature shop where visitors could buy fishing supplies. There was all the admin and paperwork associated with setting up a new company, plus the health and safety requirements associated with teaching people, including children. There was a brand to create, a digital presence to build, a launch event to plan and, of course, customers to seek out and bookings to be secured. With hardly any money to spare, I took on the vast majority of this work single-handed, propelling myself through list after list of jobs, more seeming to be added each day than I could tick off.

I did all this pushed on by the excitement of having a dream within reach, yet also quelled by a sense of unease as I sat up late on my laptop, churning through paperwork. B's occasional glances from the sofa said everything about his sense of alienation; the unspoken accusation was that I was giving all my time to the work and not enough to us. On good days, when I overcame an important obstacle and the school seemed another step closer to being a reality, I told myself that I was right to be focusing my energy where it could make a difference, that things were difficult because I was yet again busy, and it would change once I had got the school up and running. And on the bad ones, I wondered if our failing marriage was all my fault, feeling guilty that I was investing time into the school that I could be using to try to fix our problems. Perhaps if I wasn't pushing myself so hard at work, and was more present in our domestic life, we could get back to where we had been: a relationship that seemed to fit together without trying, and two people who could and did share everything.

Around the same time that I started making my first enquiries about a venue for the school, B and I had finally talked properly and admitted our problems. We were barely six months into our married life, but a vast distance had grown between us. I told him I felt unsupported by him, in both my career and social life; I would run into a wall of silence when I tried to talk about work, and was bothered by how he would sometimes refuse to accompany me to parties and events. He said that I was spending too much time away from home, and trying to run out on the country life that we had both signed up to when we moved to Yorkshire.

We were pulling hard in different directions. Yet in my mind, it was equally clear that there could be no question of giving up. Marriage was not a commitment I had made lightly. As the child of divorced parents, a girl who remembered the sharp pain of separation, I had vowed it would never happen to me. I could not look at myself in the mirror, let alone look my family and friends in the eye, if I gave up on my marriage without fighting for it. 'You have to give it time to sort out, at least a year,' my mother told me, and I knew that she was right.

So we sat, we talked and we made new vows – not the affirmations of love that are spoken at the altar, but practical details of coexistence and what we would do to better meet the other's needs: the language of a conflict being resolved rather than a union more deeply formed. Both of us pledged something: he would make more of an effort to support my work and do things with me, and I would limit my travel so that we were not apart for more than two weeks in the year. We would give ourselves at least the year my mother had advised to turn things round. Of the two most important things in my life, I was surrendering part of one to fight for the other. Accustomed to feeling certain about my choices, I had no idea if this was going to work; whether it would be the compromise that rebooted our marriage, or a career sacrifice that I would come to regret.

With just weeks to go until the launch of what we had decided to call the Northern Fishing School, I was at last beginning to feel confident. The fishery had been secured, bookings had been taken and, with the help of Swinton, a barn had been converted into an office and shop that would serve as our headquarters. After months of long days and endless worries that I had forgotten something important, the start was now in sight.

One June morning, as I prepared to place some hoops in the lake as targets for people to cast at, I realised I had not actually yet set foot in the water that was about to become my base. But I knew I already loved this lake. With its narrow shape, and the wind often cresting its surface to create the impression of a current, many visitors initially assume it to be a river. If you follow it round, through the horseshoe of connected lakes and ponds that bends around the Swinton Estate, it eventually leads to the river, feeding into the Burn as it branches out east to join the much larger Ure. For some time the lake had been little used, except for ice-skating during the winter, but I had known at first glance that it was perfect for the school: ideal for beginners, with shallow banks and no surrounding trees to disrupt someone learning how to back-cast for the first time.

Looking over the property, my contentment was boosted by the presence by my side of B, who in a conscious show of support had come over after work to help me get the site ready. As we waded in, my mind was already drifting ahead to the first classes I would give here and the exercises I would use with my students. On a good summer's day, with the sun dappling diamonds of light across the water, it would be everything I had dreamed about: a beautiful hideaway for people to escape the city, and a lake that reminded me of where I had first learned to fish. One and a half years ago I had been putting down targets like this in my front garden to prepare for the casting exam, unsure how or if I could make the dream of a fishing career happen. Now I was putting the finishing touches to my own fishing school in these beautiful surroundings.

I was dumped out of this daydream by my feet. They had hit something, far too quickly. Several more steps confirmed the fear that was burning through me. The water that was shimmering at the surface went barely any deeper. There was perhaps just a foot of it sitting on top of accumulated detritus: a thick layer of mud and leaves that had been blown over from the giant trees that guarded the nearby deer park. Our boots sank straight into the dark grey mess, deep and sticky enough that you had to twist your feet to free them. B and I just looked at each other, words hardly necessary. The first footstep was enough to know that it was bad – the rancid smell of sulphur told a story. Some further exploration, sticking our feet in at intervals up and down the lake, confirmed that the entire lake was clogged with the stuff. Because the water had been unused for several years, somehow this had gone unnoticed until now, just weeks before our grand opening.

This lake represented everything I had been building towards for years: everything I had done to drag myself from a point where I felt lost and hopeless to standing on the brink of realising my biggest ambition. All the hours I had spent by the lake in Syon Park teaching myself to fish again, all the time I had spent working on my qualifications and getting myself around the country and world to coach people, and all the big decisions to uproot my life and step into the unknown had led me to this point. But as I felt claggy mud where water should have been, all that seemed in jeopardy. In seconds I had gone from being the proud owner of a brand new fishing school to someone who didn't have a lake to cast in. How, after months of agonising over paperwork, had I neglected to check out the one fundamental thing on which my entire plan rested?

Usually I made light of my inexperience in business, telling myself that determination and enthusiasm would make up for what I didn't know. But in this moment, I felt every inch a rookie; embarrassed that I had missed such an obvious piece of due diligence and thinking how everyone who had raised an eyebrow at my ambitions would be relishing the sight of me now, run aground in the lake.

Once I had regathered myself, there was only one course of action available. I sheepishly shared the news with the team at Swinton, who kindly agreed to dredge the lake – a costly undertaking – and also offered the use of their other lakes, given this one would not now be ready until the following season. But one was not sufficiently accessible and the other was as clogged up as the first had been. We found the answer at a nearby trout fishery, where the school was based for its debut season, returning to Swinton the following year. We had recovered from a stumble, but it was a reminder that nothing worth doing is ever easy or straightforward. In fact, the more I worked to make things right, the harder everything seemed to get. The faster I ran, trying to meet every obligation and fulfil every ambition at once, the slower I seemed to go, trapped between work and home, between my marriage and my career. And the longer it went on, the less sure I became about how I was going to find my way out.

A bad day at work was made worse by the shortage of good ones at home. I would return to a house that was simmering with tension. We had lost the rhythm of our relationship, the unspoken bond that makes every decision easy and every conversation natural. Now neither of us knew how to recreate that intimacy, or even if we wanted to. At the exact time when we were supposed to be working on our problems, both of us had retreated even deeper into our own worlds. Again and again, I wondered how the man I had considered my soulmate had come to seem so distant from me. Was this really the person I had wanted to start a family with?

For months, my mind was a daily battle of powerful, colliding instincts: the knowledge that our situation had become unsalvageable, and the frustration bordering on shame that it had come to this, and so quickly. I would veer all over the place in the course of a single day. In the morning I would be determined that I was not going to let my marriage collapse, not going to fail at the most important thing I had ever tried. And by the afternoon I knew, as I had the previous day and would again the next, that it was over. It was only a question of when we would both agree to acknowledge and accept the end. We were simply two people whose expectations of life could not be contained within the shared bond of a marriage.

This was the simple but devastating truth that I tormented myself with for almost the entirety of our marriage's year-long twilight. It took a long time to accept that we had made what amounted to a terrible mistake: each of us had wrongly expected the other to adapt more to our own vision of what our future should be. We had reached a point where we were both making each other unhappy as easily as we had once fallen in love.

And as my marriage collapsed, so too did a deeply held belief about myself: that when it came to the things I truly cared about, I would do whatever it took and work as hard as I needed to succeed. Here was a failure I could not overcome through sheer determination. The prospect of divorce seemed to mock my entire approach to life. The more effort that went into this relationship, the more broken it became: carefully planned dinners revealed that we had nothing to say to each other, outings made it clear we were more distant from each other than ever.

The final months of the marriage, when it was clear that it was coming apart, were some of the most difficult of my life. It was at this point that I discovered the true meaning of loneliness – it inhabited my whole being and inhibited me in every way. Although I had plenty of support from my family and friends, I learned that no one can protect you from feelings that stalk you every waking minute, where your mind focuses a microscope on your every flaw as a person, magnifying the blame you feel and the certainty that everyone is judging you for the mistake you have made.

No one on the outside can ever know what is happening within a marriage, or how far their perceptions may be from reality. From so many sources I heard the same advice: to give it time, put in the work, know that it was not meant to be easy. I knew how it looked, a marriage ending within the course of eighteen months, but the truth was that our relationship had been faltering before we got engaged. We *had* been trying, had been doing the work, and neither of us felt even a hint that we could be happy again together.

The vast chasm between the situation as I knew it and what people were telling me to do only added to my sense of isolation. Many days I stumbled through, sometimes hardly able to form a coherent thought or to concentrate for any length of time. I couldn't see past the fog that had settled over me, a cloudy cocktail of fear, stubbornness and regret. At times this left me literally paralysed. In the car one afternoon, I was staring blankly ahead and was only alerted by the beeping behind me to the fact that the traffic light had shifted from red to green. As I tried to respond, for several long seconds I found I could move neither my hands nor feet. I was stuck in every sense: unable to go back and not sure how to move forward.

Yet I could not wallow entirely in my unhappiness. For while one important part of my life was coming to an end, another was only just beginning. After a sleepless night alone with my thoughts, I would take myself to Swinton and coach clients, doing the job I had always wanted to do, in the most perfect setting, and under a banner I could now call my own. Though hollowed out and exhausted, I was determined to present my best face to the world. The months of being pulled in two different directions, between my marriage and fishing, had helped me build the ability to compartmentalise, so that I could separate the person who felt unable to do anything

Catch

right from the one giving a confident and cheerful example to the children and first-time anglers who made up the majority of my customers at the school.

As it had before, fishing provided the comfort I needed at the time I needed it most. When I had returned from New Zealand at age twenty, teaching myself to fish again had been the hobby that gave me back the purpose and confidence I had lost. Now it was through teaching others that I found focus, absorbed by the totality of what angling requires of you. I threw myself into the all-consuming task of teaching a complex subject to people often encountering it for the first time.

As a coach, every part of the fishing process is multiplied: in addition to taking into account the water, conditions and fish, there is the person you are teaching, and your intuition for what kind of guidance they will best respond to. The student becomes almost as much of a puzzle to solve as the fish itself. Does someone want to watch and copy you, or for you to move their hands and arms to the correct position? Do they need to have their confidence boosted or their enthusiasm reined in a touch until they have grasped some overlooked detail of technique? Should they be let loose on the water now, or given a little more time practising on grass? Every day I spent applying my mind to these questions meant a few hours when it wouldn't be dominated by thoughts about my marriage. I clung to these islands of respite, moments when I felt and sounded like myself again, where I could hear the edge of confidence creeping back into my voice.

My relationship to fishing was also changing. For the five or six years since I had been a serious angler, the sport had been like an obsession to me, almost an addiction. I was single-mindedly focused on the next catch, the next qualification, the next step I could take to improve. Now that I had achieved some of those goals, my focus was starting to broaden. I was beginning to think not just about my own path through fishing, but how I could open one for other people who might never have considered picking up a rod. I was also looking at rivers not just for the movement of fish, but for where the water was lying suspiciously low, when I could smell the acrid tang of sewage that had been released from a storm drain, or see tampons and tissue paper floating by. I had started to realise that part of the unspoken act of being an angler is your duty to safeguard the rivers where you spend so much time, and which have given you so much joy. When chemical waste and rising temperatures threaten our waterways, the anglers who spend so many hours observing them are well placed to raise the alarm and support campaigns for better conservation and management. Understanding that has helped my appreciation of fishing to mature: from the relentless pursuit of the next thing to defending the fragile ecosystems on which my passion depends.

The school's first summer was a strange and dislocating time, with one part of my life breaking beyond repair while another started to take shape: the heavy recognition that my marriage would not be fixed, punctured by occasional moments of joy as I watched people catch their first fish at the school I had brought into being, all the more bitter-sweet because I knew that I could not hold on to the happiness for long.

The school gave me a release, but not the full escape I needed. I knew that our marriage could not continue. I wanted my world to be limitless, but to B that meant being rootless, a life without a home or a heart. I wanted to have it all: a never-ending exploration of new places that family life would become a part of, and all the richer for it. He believed that what we already had was better than anything we might find on horizons undiscovered, and that marriage meant building our life in Yorkshire, buying a house, and eventually adding children to the dogs. To me, his desire to settle down simply meant settling for something less than I wanted my life to be.

It was easy to see where these very contrasting ideas had stemmed from. B had his whole family and many of his friends in Yorkshire, as well as his work. He wanted to make a life in the same image, emulating the contentment and security he had always known. By contrast, I had been affected by my own itinerant upbringing and the scattering of my family. Much as a part of me wanted the stable family life in the country that I had idealised since childhood, I also craved new experiences. To me, being happy at home and seeking out adventure were two halves of the same whole, not impulses that had to be brought into conflict. But now it felt like I was being asked to choose between them.

I felt trapped by an existence in which I could predict exactly what I would be doing, with whom, a year and even a decade into the future. It was the opposite of the spontaneity I wanted, and I was never going to accept a life in which the option to move around was taken off the table. And I would not raise children in an unhappy home, nor would I give up on my ambitions to travel the world with my fishing rods, trading in my dreams to sit at home even though I was not yet in my thirties. As fishing's world of possibilities had started to open up to me, I could not accept anything being closed off.

Now the only question was when and how to extricate ourselves. I have always been someone who is better at starting things than ending them, happier when marching towards a goal than retreating from it. Here that tendency was amplified by the knowledge that the end of the marriage would mean admitting a very public failure, to all the people who had celebrated our wedding with us not two years ago.

Although I had already told my mother and closest friend that the marriage was over, in the end it took physical distance to make the separation a reality. My week in the Bolivian jungle, tracking the glints of the golden dorado in the cloudy water of the Amazon, reminded me I couldn't give up that kind of experience to stay in a relationship from which all the meaning had now drained away. It made me realise that there could be no happiness while I was trying to live without the adventure and freedom that mattered so much to me. I had already made my decision, but now I had the certainty to give voice to it.

The evening I returned, I told him: 'I can't do this any more.'

As long as the conversation that started our relationship had been, this final one before our break-up was short.

These words were all that needed to be said, though it had taken months for me to be ready to say them. That evening B packed a bag and went to stay with his mother. I knew I should feel sad, and that in time I would be confronting shame, anger and regret. But after spending so long caught between knowing and deciding, determination endlessly tussling with denial, at the moment we parted I had almost no emotions. Only the faintest stirring of relief at the thought that my life could now begin again – the flickering of a salmon's tail as it emerges from its resting place and prepares to continue the journey upstream.

RELEASE

Chapter 8

Farquhar Atoll, Seychelles.

It was one of the most exquisite places I had ever visited. Not that I was paying attention to the natural beauty surrounding me. I had stopped thinking about the Farquhar atoll behind me, a lopsided grin of green, with its rows of coconut trees and lips of perfect white sand. I had stopped noticing the sooty terns, their black crowns and charcoal feathers fluttering overhead. With the south-east trade wind blowing in my face, and our guide Gerry expertly steering the skiff with a long push pole, I gave little thought to the Aldabra giant tortoises patrolling the beaches and forest paths, and how they creep along for multiple human lifetimes in this place that seems to form its own universe, a teardrop of land alone in the Indian Ocean.

We were hunting for the one thing in this paradise that is less than picture perfect. Looking down to where the sea bed was mottled with dark bruises of coral. Searching among the landscape's many blues for the seashell-like grooves and indigo-tinged shades of a fish's tail, a corner rising from the water as it pushes its head down to feed.

This tail belongs to the bumphead parrotfish. Some fish are extraordinary for their beauty, bright colouring and sleek elegance, but not the 'bumpy'. It is a remark-ably, almost hilariously ungainly thing, like a child's drawing of an imaginary sea monster come to life. From its forehead a huge lump of pink protrudes, jutting out like a lesion against the rest of its blue-green skin. This camel-shaped hump is complemented by a donkey's buck teeth, which allow the fish to literally bite chunks out of the coral reef, and which are kept clean by tiny wrasse fish that swim straight into their mouths to work. Stuck to the side of its huge, flat body are stubby fins that you could hardly imagine being fit to swim until you see a bumphead start to run.

Bumpies are the ocean's bad dream: a fish that carries a genuine aura of menace, if you think of what the molars that can reduce hard coral to sandy dust could do to you. Ever since I had heard about them, I knew I had to tackle one. And the place to go for them would be the Seychelles, perhaps the ultimate destination for ocean fishing, where every game-fish imaginable can be found. Through the long, cold dwindling of my marriage, it was this trip I had held on to, imagining the day when I would be wading through this water, immersed in a place where there is only green behind you and endless blue ahead.

For days we had been pursuing bumpheads without success. Spotting them was not the problem, with their tails poking out of the water as they fed on the sea bed, often travelling around in schools. Nor was hooking into them. But the bumpy is a formidable opponent, making full use of the razor-sharp coral that populates its lair. I found multiple fishing lines shredded as the parrotfish dragged them out into the deeper water and along the reefs. By now I knew that, if I could land a bumphead, then one of the most anticipated catches of my life would also be one of the best-earned.

It was on our third day on Farquhar that the opportunity came: a shoal we had been following suddenly turned in our direction. They were coming closer: if they went much further they would sense our presence and flee.

'Go now, go now. Out to the right,' Gerry called out.

A long, sweeping cast. Then, during both the backward and forward motions, an extra tug on the line to load the rod and increase the speed of the stroke: a double haul, the saltwater angler's best friend. My orange crab fly dangled in front of the fish, and I gave the line a few gentle pulls, but no firm strips that might have spooked this terrifyingly aggressive yet easily scared monster. Then I waited a few seconds to see if it would bite.

'It's on,' Gerry said with excitement.

The fish had taken, and my rod was arching out like a ship's prow, reel screaming as the fish tore out line in its flight. The rod bent and the pole glided through the water as Gerry steered our boat through the flats, expertly ushering my bumpy away from the coral. I braced with both feet. No fish I'd encountered, not even the giant trevally, had ever run as fast or hard as this, ripping a full length of line straight through and taking me to my backing – the thinner material used to load up the reel and give you extra capacity, but only meant for actual fishing as a last resort.

The tug is the drug.

With the bumphead on my line, feeling the raw power of the fish and the breeze in my face, letting the humidity hug me close as the voices around me shouted advice, I finally felt like myself again. No doubts or questions, regrets and recriminations. Just the simplicity of the water and a fishing line at full tilt, my arms straining and mouth suddenly dry with tension. The only thoughts in my head: to hold on, brace myself, and gradually start reeling this majestic monster in. This was where I belonged, where I was always meant to be. As I squeezed the rod, feeling the parrotfish start to come under my control, I knew that in this distant place I had come home: back to travel, back to adventure, back to fishing without limits and life without regrets. This time, with both hands gripping tight, there was no danger of me letting go.

The Atlantic salmon that has migrated home from the ocean, fully grown and ready to begin its run upstream, has beaten overwhelming odds to come this far. Yet many of the return leg's greatest perils still lie ahead. Rejoining the river and swimming back up to the spawning grounds may be one of the shortest parts of this epic journey, but dangers lurk at every turn: bottlenose dolphins that patrol the Moray Firth, bullying the salmon into shallow water to hunt; seals that gather in dozens on the estuary's sand banks, waiting to scoop up any salmon that mistimed their passage when the tide was too low; and upstream, otters that lurk above waterfalls, knowing that if they lie in wait for long enough, a leaping salmon will be delivered straight to them for their next meal.

The returning salmon that can avoid being consumed whole by a predator several times its size faces the risk of a much smaller foe: sea lice, beetle-shaped parasites that attach themselves to the skin of the salmon and feed off its blood and skin. There is nothing new about these creatures, but their prevalence has been markedly increased by the salmon farming industry.

Compared to their wild cousins, these farmed fish have lived lives of almost total confinement, grown from harvested salmon eggs in tanks, caged lakes and ultimately sea farms – giant floating nets up to two hundred metres wide that allow the water to flow in while stopping the salmon from getting out. So confined, the fish are condemned to swim round and round in circles for up to two years until they are slaughtered. Whereas the wild salmon's flesh grows pink through a diet of crustaceans, the farmed equivalent would be grey without the chemicals that are injected into their feed. Meanwhile interbreeding between wild and farmed fish is thought to be weakening the unique genetics that make the former such a rugged survivor.

The cramped pens also provide a rich environment for sea lice. The fish that fall prey to them will suffer a gruesome death, found at the bottom of the pens, their heads raw and exposed – eaten alive by hundreds of lice that have stripped away the skin in their hunger to feed on the blood.

Even the wild Atlantic salmon don't escape; they must swim past these farms, through chemical-infused and sometimes lice-infested water. Often they emerge with parasites crawling all over their bodies. Even if these are not numerous enough to be fatal, they can weaken the salmon, affecting its chances of surviving or successfully breeding. Salmon farming is just one more barrier between the migrating salmon and the upstream ending to its story.

It was late, and drink had been taken, when the challenge was handed down, one I was in no mood to refuse.

'Bet you can't beat me.'

The accent was treacle-thick Texas. The location a lodge in the north of Argentina. Watching this exchange a little nervously was my mother.

Welcome to the world of fishing. The sport brings together people who you could never otherwise imagine in the same room, as likely to be heart surgeons as tree surgeons, who may have nothing in common except their desire to spend the day by the water, and the evening talking about catches made and lost. The universal language of angling transcends all barriers of age, culture or background. On the common ground of fishing, the conversations start immediately, and they rarely stop until the trip is over.

Normally personal best catches would have been the topic of discussion, but that night we had turned to a different form of competition. In the nearby games room I had spotted a pool table and, fortified by a little Argentinian red wine, started talking up my skills. Only when I actually stepped up to the table with my Texan challenger, who held the cue like a matchstick, did I realise that the table was considerably larger than the ones I was used to in pubs back home.

'What's the wager?'

Southern voices turned to cheers as one of their number came back into the room and opened his cupped hands to reveal a stag beetle. I took in the skeleton, ridged along its back like armour plating, and began to feel queasy as I watched its antennae twitch. The loser would be enjoying this morsel as an hors d'oeuvre. Suddenly the pool table started looking very large indeed. Now I really had to win: I was not putting that thing anywhere near my mouth. And to my surprise it turned out to be all the motivation I needed; I sank ball after ball as if I was casting and not cueing.

As I potted the black ball in the final frame, I shouted with relief, 'I win!'

I drank in the moment, my mother trying not to laugh as our good-natured companion bit into the beetle, and the cheering resumed as it released a hideous-looking white gunk.

I felt more than relief. This trip, the first since my separation from B, was a release and an escape I desperately needed (it would soon be followed by several others, including the pursuit of bumpheads in the Seychelles). For several winter months I had sat alone in our house, dealing with the practicalities of untangling my life from his, and agonising over the question of whether I could and should stay in Yorkshire.

There were so many reasons to leave. Not just in search of a new start, but because the impending divorce was making me a stranger, even an outcast, in my adopted home. B had been the one with roots here: our friends in the area had started out as his, and they went back to being so.

By now we had exhausted any possibility of reconciliation. From the opposite end of a marriage counsellor's sofa, he had left me in no doubt that the relationship he wanted was one I could not live with. 'No trips abroad, no salmon trips to Scotland.'

I sat silently, wondering how I could have ever fallen in love with someone who wanted to strip away so much of the meaning in my life – large parts of my career, my passion, even my childhood memories. It confirmed, if confirmation was still needed, that my travelling had not been the problem so much as his yearning for someone who would devote themselves to him and his vision: something it should have been clear I would never do without also having the opportunity to travel in pursuit of the work and play I loved.

I knew that this would be the narrative of events: that I had walked out on him, always putting myself and my career before the marriage. That I had been the one to blame. This would become the accepted version. Friends I had met through him stopped talking to me. One even blanked me in public, passing me in a supermarket car park without a second look when I waved. Events took a comical turn when a rumour made its way back to me that I had been having an affair. I worked out that this had been started by someone who had seen the regular appointments in my diary with a sponsor and drawn creative conclusions.

But even as I became alienated from my home, leaving was not straightforward. Much as I desperately wanted to start my life again beyond the shadow of my divorce, the fishing school was pulling me back. The decision loomed over me, but I was in no state to make it. The only thought I could form was that I needed to get away, to put as much distance between me and the previous year as possible.

That was when I messaged a friend who I knew could help. I wanted to go to Argentina, to fish for sea trout and to take my mum. The response was almost immediate.

'I'll be there in February. Meet me in Buenos Aires, I'll arrange the rest.'

Stephan was an established figure in the industry: one part guide, one part photographer, pursuits he brought together through the media company he ran, creating content for fishing brands and destinations. We had first met several years before, when I was starting my fishing career. He had the kind of life I had sometimes daydreamed about, on what felt like a constant global tour of the best fishing spots in the world, work funding play.

With his help, fishing in Argentina proved to be everything I had hoped for. On the Menendez, a tributary of the Rio Grande, the river is narrow and the land rolls flat and featureless. Only the roaming of guanacos (Argentinian llamas) and beavers pawing along the banks can disturb the almost desolate solitude. Between you and the fat, sea-run trout stands the unfettered wind, a curse for the unwary caster but an aid to those who learn how to master it. Soon we were used to the lower trajectory needed to take the line back over the open plains and catch the gust, supercharging the distance of the cast. And after multiple small catches, I finally landed what I had come for: a sixteen-pound monster. A fish I knew I would never forget, as I took in its chessboard of silver skin and dark spots. It had been one of my final casts on the penultimate day of the trip, with the disc-shaped sun hanging low and huge.

I had come for the fishing, for the chance to fix my head and spend time with my mother. I hadn't bargained for what the holiday turned into. It had been a few years since we had seen one another, and as soon as we arrived in Buenos Aires we started geeking out about fishing.

Like so many fishing conversations, it simply went on and on, from the side of the hotel pool in Buenos Aires right through the two weeks we spent fishing in Argentina. During all that time, Stephan and I seemed to be the only ones not noticing how much time we were spending in each other's company, to the point where the girl he was with, an acquaintance from Bolivia complained to my mother that he was ignoring her. But when Mum asked me towards the end of the trip if I was interested in him, I could not have been more clear.

'Absolutely not. He's *crazy*.'

Over years of long-distance friendship, Stephan had spared no details in describing his romantic as well as angling exploits: a girlfriend 'ghosted' in one part of the world while another was 'zombied' (revived) several time zones away. I knew that, as well as being one of the best fishermen I had met, he was the last person who could be considered boyfriend material; he was as platonic a friend as it was possible to imagine. Not to mention that it was just months after the breakdown of my marriage, and I hadn't even thought about another relationship.

At the end of the trip we both went home, he to Germany and I back to Yorkshire. I thought it might be several more years before our paths crossed again. Then the next day he messaged me, while I was walking Sedge on the familiar path round the neighbouring fields, past the blackthorn bushes that would soon be coming into season: 'I need a copy of your passport, I'm taking you somewhere for a week. Say yes.' Having just had a taste of my regained freedom, I needed no encouragement to make another trip. Crunching through the late-winter frost, I could feel the tingle of excitement that had been gone from my life for too long – of not knowing where I was going to be next week, or a year from now. With one fresh adventure behind me and another around the corner, the pain of an ending was giving way to the hope of a new beginning.

The tug was epic, so sudden and firm that I could hardly believe it was a salmon on the end of my line. Here none of the usual rules of salmon fishing seemed to apply – no careful pause, no God Save the Queen. Just a take and a run that sent the line humming out of the reel, at a buzz-saw speed that made me instinctively snatch my fingers out of the way. 'It's a *psycho*,' I heard myself calling, knowing that there was nothing to do except hold on and wait for the intensity of the sprint to burn out.

People had told me that salmon fishing in Russia is different. Compared to Western waters, which have seen numbers decline steeply over recent decades, Russia hosts an Atlantic salmon population of almost vast abundance: just one of its rivers, the Ponoi, sees around 50,000 spawners return to its waters each year, almost ten times more than are caught annually on the Spey in Scotland. Russia's vast and remote waters are one of the last places in the world where salmon populations remain relatively free from the march of pollution, aquafarming and climate change. Both the number of fish and the remote locations of the rivers means that, unlike Scottish salmon, these are creatures untouched by man as well as protected by nature. Your fly is likely to be the first they have ever seen, with none of the inbuilt wariness that comes from consistent exposure to fishing. These fish are feisty, they are strong and they bite the fly more like trout than salmon.

The pursuit of Russian salmon is as hardcore as the battle to bring them in. Fishing the Kola Reserve, on the eastern edge of the Murmansk Oblast, which borders Finland, we had been on our feet all day wading, climbing up canyons, slogging through tundra and clambering over boulders. With one eye on the ground in front of me, the other kept returning to the middle of the river, looking for the big sunken boulders that produce areas of slack water behind and in front: a perfect resting place for the salmon that has paused its run upstream. The ideal quarry for the angler.

Then I spotted one. On the first cast it took and suddenly I was in the kind of intense battle that felt more like a saltwater giant than an Atlantic salmon. When the fish finally came in, Stephan identified it and explained why: this was an *osenka,* plump, bright silver and extra strong. And for good reason; in a month or two's time, winter would arrive, the river would freeze over and the salmon would wait it out under the ice, before completing its run the following spring and spawning in autumn. Even by the hardy standards of the species, these freeze-proof salmon are true warriors and born survivors.

My tussle with the *osenka* was just one of the many marvels of our trip to the Kola Peninsula, whose rivers are so distant that we needed a helicopter to access them, the ride giving a peerless view of the forest and tundra that seems to stretch out for ever, brown bears and reindeer running through them, tomato-bright red moss cutting through the familiar autumnal shades of yellow, brown and green. We followed the valleys that have been cut by countless years of meltwater, spawning streams and creeks that eventually lead into the magnificent

Kola Reserve, Russia.

rivers themselves, sometimes a hundred or even two hundred metres wide. And this was just the autumn spectacle. In the winter the sun hardly rises to disrupt the deep blankets of snow, and during the violent summer it seems never to set, allowing for the enticing possibility of midnight fishing.

On the Ponoi itself, with deep breaths of mist rising from the water and only pine trees on either side for company, it can feel as though you have not so much arrived in a new place as departed the planet altogether. Even knowing that this is a popular destination for anglers, you can believe that you might be the first person ever to have cast a line into this wilderness. It was here that I caught a huge cock salmon, its tail like a merman's, with patches of pale, red-spotted flesh on its bronze body, like fragments of a Renaissance fresco clinging to a church ceiling.

It was over eighteen months since I had received Stephan's request for my passport. That was late February 2020 and, along with everyone else in the world, my life was about to change. His mystery destination had been Venezuela, a trip abandoned as the certainty of a lock-down approached. We took what proved to be the final flight out of Caracas and I went with him to Croatia, to stay at his family's house for what was meant to be a week. With travel shutting down it ended up being two months, with much of our time spent wandering through the Old Town of Dubrovnik, its churches and palaces deserted. On this walled thumb of land that pokes its limestone buildings and rust-coloured roofs into the Adriatic, I felt as cut off from the world as I had in the most remote places I had been fishing – and glad to be so.

By then I had started to see what my mother had suggested back in Argentina. With Stephan I had found someone who I never wanted to stop talking to, and with whom I had the security of knowing there would be no surprises. We already knew one another as friends, we respected each other's work, and our lives seemed to mesh as if designed, making trips together when we could and pursuing our own work independently when needed.

For the first time I felt like I was with someone who truly understood me, who would stop the car when we encountered a hedgehog crossing the road, knowing that I wanted to move it into the hedgerow and to safety. In so many past relationships I had always felt like I had to explain myself, as if we didn't quite share a common language. Stephan was the first boyfriend who seemed entirely in step with me, and frequently a little ahead. Unlike most relationships, where falling in love comes before getting to know each other, we started from a point where there were no hidden secrets or unspoken truths.

After the travel restrictions were lifted, he came back with me to the UK. Seeing him and Sedge together, like old friends even though they were meeting for the first time, felt like the final confirmation that we were doing the right thing.

Being with Stephan also meant combining our wanderlust. That winter, just before Christmas of 2020, we found ourselves pike fishing in Rügen, an island clinging to the north-east coast of Germany, a place of iron skies, brackish water and unforgiving Arctic winds.

For me the pike was a hobby fish, one I liked to pursue but would never guide others to catch. It also felt like my nemesis: whenever I went pike fishing, I would make catches but the big one would always find a way of eluding me. Every time I mentioned this to Stephan he said that we had to go to Rügen, where pike converge to feed on migratory fish including herring, helping them grow into the biggest of their species in the world. If I wanted to get my metre-long pike, we had to come here. And it had to be in winter, when the pike swim inland to feed in advance of their spring spawning season, bringing them into wading distance of the shore.

With my seven layers and bag of bobble hats, I thought I was ready for water I knew would be the coldest I had yet encountered. I was ready for a little suffering in order to add a personal best pike to my collection. But nothing could have prepared me for the Baltic Sea in December: the fog descended like a shroud, my feet were blocks of ice inside my waders and the wind seemed to turn any pair of gloves I wore into tissue paper. Nor was this a quick dip in the freezing ocean. We fished almost every day for three weeks, from early morning until darkness was threatening. It rained, hailed and snowed. At the end of the trip, Stephan had frostbite in his toes. Still we waded on, a ceaseless search for shoals of bait fish that could lead us to pike. On those long days the whole world felt monochrome and I tried to fill my head with water depths, fly patterns and casting strokes while my whole body inwardly howled against the cold.

If proof was ever needed that fishing can be more addiction than passion, that trip provided it. Like all great loves, the love of fishing can easily tip from adoration into obsession: a pursuit that is capable of freeing the mind from normal concerns can also focus it to the point of myopia, where catching the fish you have fixed on becomes all that matters, and it doesn't matter how long it takes, how cold it gets, or what else you are supposed to be doing. Each evening I would complain to Stephan that I couldn't feel my fingers or toes even after several hours out of the water, and then each morning this would all be forgotten as we went out with new plans and fresh approaches, my only thought for the fish I was yet to catch. The idea of a metre-long pike had me hooked.

Still it eluded me. I caught several that exceeded ninety centimetres, and admired the unique snakeskin patterning of each fish and its hundreds of icicle-like teeth, but none that hit the magic metre.

After twenty days of back-to-back fishing we had to go home, and by then even my determination had been sapped by the relentless conditions. 'I just want to enjoy my life again,' I moaned, teeth chattering, before laughing misty breath into the air as I heard how ridiculous I sounded.

In a wider sense I already was. I had begun the year alone at home, recently separated and not knowing what to do next. Now, having spent it in all sorts of unexpected places, some planned and others not, I was ending it with Sedge and with Stephan, my new partner, in a Yorkshire winter that felt almost mild after the Baltic chill, my love of travelling the world to fish renewed, and with a second season at the fishing school completed around pandemic restrictions.

As we were preparing for a solitary Covid Christmas, an email arrived: my signed divorce papers. Over a year after our separation, the parting was officially complete. It felt like a symbolic moment to sum up how far I had come, from the despair of feeling lost and alone, trapped in what was meant to be the most meaningful relationship of my life, to the freedom offered by a new path opening up, one with no limits on where I could go or what I could do. What might have been a melancholy moment in fact gave me hope, confirming that I could now put the past behind me and embrace the future that was already beginning to take shape.

Chapter 9

The Swinton Estate, North Yorkshire.

The pandemic had been a major challenge for the school, but we had managed to navigate it successfully. We had adapted our teaching methods to accommodate social distancing and other safety measures, and we had even managed to offer some online courses.

Despite the challenges, the school had continued to grow and thrive.

As I packed my bags, I was proud of what we had accomplished, and I was excited to see what the future held.

This time it was for a three-month trip around South America, taking in fishing landmarks including Brazil for peacock bass and back to Argentina to fish for sea trout, dorado, brown trout and monster rainbow trout. I knew how lucky I was to be embarking on another journey to a place I had dreamed of going, but I was also feeling stressed and burned out, unable to remember when I had last properly stopped or envisage when I could again, and as close as I get to being fed up with my lot. I had been on a high, with the feeling that my life was back on track and my business was now established. Now a hangover was here, as I started to take for granted things I had once strived for, and began to feel the attrition of years in which I had hardly stopped to rest. Even during lockdown, when much of my work ground to a halt, I had made myself busy by starting up Cancer and Pisces, a charity that would function as a fishing club for those living with cancer and their carers.

My stress must have been transferring itself to the companion who never left my side, Sedge. Like a miniature sentry, he accompanied me both at home and on the riverbank. But now, even more than usual, he was clinging to me, following me from room to room as I roamed the flat pulling together different bits of kit to pack away. He had seen the massive bags before, and knew they signified that we were soon to be apart. As usual, while I was away he would be staying with friends who loved him and whose dogs he knew. It was a wrench to leave him, but I comforted myself that he would be safe and happy in a familiar home. I spent every spare minute cuddling him on the sofa, trying to comfort the anxiety that mirrored my own.

Right before I was due to depart, I came down to London for a meeting of the Cancer and Pisces trustees. My attention was being pulled in all different directions as I thought about last-minute preparations as well as the drive south and the following evening's event. It didn't help when I turned up at the dry-cleaners to discover that, because I had left my clothing there for a week too long, they had given it away. I spent half the journey to

London complaining about this to my mum, who was accompanying me to the dinner, she was upset that one of the lost items had been a vintage piece of hers. I felt a little better when we arrived in south London and parked on a quiet, dimly lit one-way street. I got out to unpack our bags and Sedge, who would normally have waited until he was called, slipped out of my open door. Mum intercepted him and put him back in the car, but somehow, while we were fussing over the pile of bags, he got out again. She was asking where Sedge was, and I was saying I thought she had put him in the car, and we were both calling out to him when it happened.

The street had been completely deserted since we arrived. There were few streetlights and no passing pedestrians or traffic. But then one car appeared, seemingly from nowhere, like a portent in a dream. It was going fast and I remember shutting my eyes as it passed us, as if trying to block out what I knew might happen. And then I heard an almost gentle thud. The car had flashed to the end of the street in a few seconds and I heard Sedge yelp, a brief, single screech like the sound of a saw meeting metal.

Suddenly the street was not quiet at all. I was running after Sedge, screaming his name. He, too, was running, showing no obvious signs of serious injury. Someone appeared at the end of the road and I called out for them to stop him from getting further away. Eventually I reached Sedge and found a quiet place to lay him down.

I was frantically running my hands over his body, searching for bleeding, but all I could feel was a lump on his groin. He was completely noiseless. Normally, whether in happiness or distress, he would be going crazy about even the smallest thing. One thing I had almost never known my dog to be was silent.

As Sedge lay quiet, the scene around us became progressively busier. People were coming out of their houses, bringing blankets and calling up local vets to see who was nearest and still open. There were fragments of almost bizarre conversation – one man approached to ask if he was friendly and I heard myself saying I didn't know because I didn't know how hurt he was. Then at some point the driver of the car appeared, asking if the dog was ok and in the same breath saying that he hadn't actually been driving that fast. Although I have thought, many times since, about what I would like to have said to him, at that moment I voiced nothing. I didn't point out how recklessly he had been driving or how mendacious it was to argue that, having been going too fast to stop after the collision, he could conceivably have been within the 20mph limit. Like my dog I was in a near-silent state of panic, completely focused on Sedge and recognising that no amount of screaming or recriminations would help him. Sedge too was drained of his normal bubbly energy. Both of us seemed to realise how serious this was.

During this strange scene with people gathered around, time seemed to stretch on and on, but in reality we had got Sedge back into the car and to the vet within about twenty minutes of the incident. The vet, in a gentle Antipodean accent, told me that the main concern was brain injury from the head collision; his blood pressure was fine and he hadn't broken any bones. But one eye was responding slower than the other, and, unusually, a little piece of his tongue was sticking out from between his teeth. He said the next twelve hours would be crucial: if Sedge made it through to the morning, his chances would be good.

Having existed in an eerie state of calm since Sedge was hit, I started to wobble while talking to the receptionist at the surgery. The shock was ebbing away and in its place were starting to come the hundred questions. How had it happened? Why hadn't I been keeping a closer eye on him? Why didn't I have a cage in the car for him to travel safely in? With a practised kindness he consoled me: no one can be paying attention to their dog the whole time; they slip leads, run ahead of their owners or out of open doors all the time. Sometimes accidents just happen and there is nothing you can do to prevent it.

After being told that I was not allowed to accompany Sedge to the animal hospital where he would be taken overnight, I reluctantly returned to the friends' house where we were staying and sat down for dinner with the family. I was trying to hold myself together, but was in a state of panic, running through the incident over and over in my head, asking myself what I could or should have done differently. The thought that I might lose him, one that had visited me fleetingly during a severe allergic episode he had had months earlier, now crashed over me with full force.

I did not have to endure the agony of waiting for much longer. Before the dinner had broken up, my phone rang and I immediately knew what it must be. Sedge had barely made it to the hospital; he had suffered a seizure as he was being carried through the door, and died of a brain haemorrhage. 'We just couldn't do anything,' the gentle voice on the phone said. 'I'm so sorry.'

Sedge was not the first animal I had loved and lost. But nothing could have prepared me for the experience of having him torn away from me, the manner of his death, or the timing. Although I had rescued Sedge, I always felt the truth of our relationship was that he saved me, his paw prints indelibly etched into my defining years. He came into my life as it was undergoing one of its biggest changes; then, as the consequences of that choice unravelled, he consoled and comforted me, with the wordless loyalty that only a dog can provide. He was my companion and my guardian, obsessively by my side at all times. On long journeys, during late nights and early mornings, at home and on the road, Sedge was always there, always utterly himself, always dementedly attentive to me. He barked like mad every time I netted a fish and, after his latest furious and futile pursuit of a squirrel, would think nothing of throwing himself into a fast-running river and swimming across it to regain his place alongside me. In the darkest days after my divorce, when I became almost paranoid about what every other person thought of me, cuddling with Sedge was one of the few ways I could comfort myself. He was with me through multiple house moves, a wedding and a divorce, business ups and downs, and countless trips around the country to see friends who loved him almost as much as I did.

I think about him every day and cannot believe he is gone. When I shut my eyes I can still see him leaping out of the river, water dripping from his dark nose, barking his greeting – a joyful, generous soul who lived his best life and gave more to mine than I ever could have imagined.

If anyone outside of fishing is familiar with a part of the wild salmon's life cycle, it is the 'run': the final upstream leg of its journey, returning it to the spawning grounds of its birth, complete with the tourist attraction of salmon leaping over falls as they fight against the current to achieve their purpose. Yet the very idea of a 'salmon run' implies a whole series of things that the culminating stage of this marathon journey is not. In reality the upstream migration is not quick; it takes many months and occupies several distinct stages. It is not a race, for, although salmon are competing with each other to breed, they are also following a path set by numerous intrinsic factors, independent of their peers. And it is not singular; some salmon enter their natal river in the spring, many months before they will breed, and others follow through the summer and autumn.

Like all other aspects of the salmon's life, the run is a complex and much-studied phenomenon that contains a high degree of variation and uncertainty. There are 'early' rivers in which salmon can be expected to start running during the spring months, 'late' ones where fish will not usually be seen until September and October, and multiple alternatives in between, as well as waters that see fish returning throughout the season. The timing and duration of the run may depend on the length and flow of the river, the genetic predisposition of the salmon, and the length of time they have spent out at sea; those that have spent multiple winters away typically begin the journey home in advance of the grilse that have been gone for just one. Tidal patterns, onshore winds, hormone levels, water temperature and daylight hours all have a role to play in determining exactly when the salmon begins the critical final leg of its journey.

Memory, smell and magnetism have helped to bring the salmon back to its beginning, with an unerring certainty that is the signature of the species. The purpose of the fish is clear and its navigation almost astoundingly reliable. Yet for all the salmon's dogged certainty, its arrival back in familiar fresh water does not, typically, spur a rush upstream. Especially for spring and summer arrivals, there are months to kill until the waters will be cool enough for breeding, whose time will not arrive until October at the earliest. Many will take the opportunity to 'lie up' in deep pools some way downstream of the spawning grounds. Here they become the sphinx-like quarry of anglers who obsess over how to attract the interest of a fish that has no need to feed, and no incentive to rise to meet their fly. They are recovering from the stresses of the journey so far but also resting for the exertions ahead of them. Despite how far they have already come, the pinnacle of their work still remains ahead.

The sky was grey over the trees at Swinton. With a semicircle of guests gathered around our instructor Charlie, it seemed like an ordinary day at the Northern Fishing School as we entered our fourth season in the spring of 2022. But this was not just another group of students, mixing novices with those who had fished a little before. It was another new beginning, of something that had been more than a year in the planning. And despite the distinct lack of sunshine, I thought I had never seen the place look so beautiful as we laid down targets, ran through circuits of casting exercises on the grass, and finally began to fish.

This was the first meeting of the Cancer and Pisces Trust, which had begun as an idea more than a year earlier. I had been sent a book, the memoir of Mick May, a City professional and fly fisherman, who had been living for almost a decade with mesothelioma, a cancer affecting the lining of the lung, which has a median survival time of just ten months. He had written the book, whose name we adopted for the charity, about how fishing had been one of his main sources of therapy.

Every word he had written about fishing, and its ability to bring peace in the face of overwhelming life events, made sense to me. I had started the school because I wanted to introduce more people to the joy and serenity of angling, and was immediately attracted by the thought of extending this to those facing some of the worst days of their lives. Moreover, the benefits of fishing for cancer sufferers, in both physical and psychological terms, were already well established: the casting action is a good way of rebuilding muscle tone in the back and arms, the pursuit of angling is one that absorbs your available attention to the exclusion of all else, and by its nature fishing provides a platform for conversation, for people going through serious illness to share the confidences and ask the difficult questions that seem to come more easily by the water, rod in hand.

Mick's book hit home. It expressed everything I had always known about fishing's ability to provide both comfort and purpose, how that magical combination of being in nature, developing an exacting skill and feeling the joy of making a catch can lighten the soul like nothing else. Sharing that with others had been part of my motivation since the beginning, all the way back to running casting sessions in Green Park when nobody in the industry knew me and I had no qualifications to do so. It had informed all the most important steps on my fishing journey, from putting myself through the casting instructor exam so I could become the best possible guide and teacher, to setting up the school so I could bring together both those who already loved angling and others who might be experiencing it for the first time. Now my focus was increasingly turning outwards, to what I could use my platform and my business to achieve, and how I could fulfil that original mission to spread the angling gospel. As wonderful as fishing is, you have to know it to love it, and for many it seems too complicated and inaccessible to consider. People think you have to be a particular kind of person: quiet, patient and contemplative. In fact, fishing is equally open to extroverts, and, while it does take a little patience to get used to the fundamentals of technique, angling itself is anything but slow and steady: you are constantly considering where to cast, whether to switch your fly, and if you have just seen a telling hint moving through the water. Your mind can never stop working. But fishing's old-fashioned image is difficult to shake off, and I have always wanted everything I do in the industry to combat that perception and encourage people to give it a try.

Using the school as a base to host fishing days for cancer patients and survivors felt like a chance to further that and, in a small way, pay forward a little of the good that fishing had done for me. Before I had fully considered what setting up something like this would involve, indeed before I had even finished Mick's book, I was talking to him on the phone about it.

The requirements of setting up the charity meant that, even though we worked quickly, a project that had been conceived in the early months of 2021 did not launch until the following year's fishing season. On that beautifully grey May morning, when we welcomed the first Cancer and Pisces fishing group, the huddle of a dozen people felt like so much more than just another cohort of students. They were the first of many who we hope will experience the magic of fishing, perhaps at its most powerful when it can provide a distraction from the worst things in life. The immersive qualities of fishing – its unique blend of ups and downs, joys and frustrations, introspection and community – can provide an escape like little else.

For all the warm feeling as we got down to work, the launch was also a deeply poignant day defined by an absence – that of Mick himself. Over the previous winter, as we were putting final preparations in place, his health had been deteriorating, even as he continued to work on the project. He passed away in the first week of March, at home. Having faced the reality that he might only live a year after being diagnosed, he described this almost-decade as the best years of his life.

There was no better advocate than Mick for the deep meaning of fishing in the lives of those who love it: not just as a sporting pursuit but as a whole series of personal journeys destined never to be completed – in search of the next catch, the perfect casting action, the personal best, the undiscovered river and, above all, the sensation of the line going taut as a fish takes the fly. The intoxicating feeling that drags you back in search of another hit. Through the Cancer and Pisces Trust, we want to encourage people to see, as so many have before them, how the joys of life can feel richer and the trials more manageable when you are standing waist-deep in water, rod in hand.

The iconic image of the salmon is one that occurs near the end of its continent-crossing migration. To reach the high points of the river that play host to the prime spawning grounds they must first overcome its most formidable features, chief among them the waterfall. It seems an absurdly uneven contest: up to a few metres of steeply banked rock against a fish that is just a few dozen inches long, with no obvious physiology to help it spring upwards.

Yet the salmon has not swum thousands of miles and lived through so many risks to be discouraged by the need for aerobatics. The urgency to return to its birthplace has carried it this far, and now it summons that determination to overcome one of its final obstacles. The fish that has spent years swimming must now show that, for one critical moment, it is capable of flying. Using the upward current created by the water crashing downwards into the plunge pool, the salmon propels itself, tail flapping madly, able to jump as high as twelve feet into the air. If it fails and is slapped back down by the falling water, it tries again, resting and leaping until the job has been done.

For those that make it, the gravity-defying leap is a final display of determination and defiance in a life that has been defined by these things. Nature seems almost to laugh in the face of the salmon who has come all this way to be presented with what must appear an insurmountable barrier. Yet this remarkable creature, conditioned for survival and compelled to progress in the face of overwhelming odds, pays it no heed. It continues towards the destination where it started, the hen to dig her redd and the cock to fight for its place in the hierarchy that will determine breeding rights.

The spawning is a culmination, but not necessarily an ending. Hens, which can shed more than a fifth of their body weight in the course of disgorging thousands of eggs as they spawn, may live to become kelts who return to complete the migratory circle a second time, and even in rare instances a third or fourth. The telltale scale markings signify the ultimate survivors of this hardy species, who can live for over a decade as they swim from river to sea and back, again and again. Kelts do not just live to see another season and spawn again; they also play a disproportionate role in the fertility of the species, being responsible for a higher share of eggs than their numbers alone would suggest.

Even for the majority of salmon, who expire after spawning through some combination of exhaustion, disease and predation, the story of their lives is not quite complete. Their carcasses help to promote insect life in the spawning grounds as they decay, contributing towards the availability of food for the offspring whose emergence from the redd they will not live to witness. The river claims its own, and another cycle turns in the endless circle of life. Even in death, the salmon makes one last contribution to the purpose its existence has been dedicated to: the survival of its species.

Chapter 10

*The Agua Boa, an upper tributary
of the Amazon River, Brazil.*

On the Agua Boa in northern Brazil, you are as far from worldly concerns as it seems possible to be. A shimmering sheet of glass cut into sandy banks, this offshoot of the Amazon River is bracketed by trees, with only the screeching, clicking, chattering chorus above to disturb the calm. It is as though calm, green-tinged water has been poured into the cauldron of the Brazilian rainforest. And through it moves a fittingly beautiful fish: the peacock bass, its golden-brown skin decorated with a whole host of plumages: bars, blotches, stripes and spots that denote the different varieties of a fish that fights with a pride its appearance demands – jumping, running and writhing, a creature of the river with the sensibilities of a sea fish.

Pursuing this fish, in this place, was something I had long wanted; a picture that had become increasingly vivid as Stephan and I planned this trip to take us down the spine of South America. But now we were here, I could not lose myself in a setting that should have felt all-encompassing. Cutting through the clear water on the boat, my mind was still on that dimly lit London street, hearing the screech of the car, my dog's solitary yelp and the gentle voice of the vet on the phone.

Our bags were already packed for this trip, but after Sedge died I wondered if I could or should still go. But no thought felt worse in that moment than having to go home to Yorkshire, to a house where every corner held a memory of him, and where I knew I would only sit staring at open doors, waiting for him to trot through them.

I knew I should be fishing, wanted to, but over long days in the sticky heat frequently found myself struggling. As if pushing away a favourite meal, I could not face the water, summon the concentration to track the peacocks through its clear depths, or make myself worry about whether I had the right fly pattern tied on. Every now and then Stephan would put the rod in my hands and I would cast, but I was not in fishing mode; I was unable to give myself to the pursuit or to let the water fill my mind to the exclusion of all else. So often fishing had been the therapy I needed, but the loss of Sedge was too recent, too raw to allow me to escape even in this secluded spot.

As the trip went on, we fished ever more remote locations. On our last day in Brazil before heading down to Argentina, we went upstream of our lodge outside Manaus until we were hacking our way through the trees to reach a lagoon that felt like the rainforest's secret garden, its clear waters high and brimming with peacock bass and redtail catfish, leopard-printed on top and milky white underneath, their long whiskers like miniature walrus tusks. It was one of the most compelling places I had ever fished, sight-casting at fish that had risen towards the surface and following them as they tried to flee into the anonymity of the jungle. The peacock bass is famously responsive to noise; a fly popped onto the water is almost enough to guarantee a bite. In just half a day, we caught and released over eighty fish, each of them displaying its own distinctive pattern. Yet even caught up in this frenzy of casting, hooking and playing what felt like a fish every other minute, I could not stop thinking about Sedge. So entwined had he become in my fishing life that it was impossible to be on the water and not feel the bitterness of his loss. All I could think about was that I would never again experience his presence, the expectant look as I packed my bags to go away or his bark of acknowledgement as I brought a trout or salmon into the net. Sedge, who had so religiously stayed by my side during life, was now a memory stalking me as I struggled to reconcile myself to the idea that he had gone for ever.

As we fished for some of the largest rainbow trout in the world on Patagonia's Jurassic Lake, and gigantic golden dorado on the Upper Paraná River, I didn't know if anything could change my mood. But when the owner of the lodge casually mentioned that their dog had had puppies, and asked if we wanted to meet them, I immediately felt something. It was the sight of these newborns, little golden, black and brown tennis balls with their eyes not yet opened, that gave me my first dose in weeks of unspoiled happiness. Then I looked at the mother, exhausted from the effort of birthing and rearing her babies in the punishing heat, looking like she was the one who needed nursing. Soon I was visiting them every morning after we woke up and every evening when we returned from the river.

It should have been too soon after losing Sedge to spend time with other dogs, but I found comfort in the beautiful innocence of these puppies, watching their mother tend them and feeling as if nature was replacing some part of what it had lost. Although attached to the lodge, these were roaming street dogs that went where they pleased, and the mother had her work cut out protecting her pups from the giant lizards that stalked the area, digging holes for them to sit in and constantly moving them around below the surrounding buildings. I couldn't have known that this was what I needed, but having something to look after, bringing her food and water each morning, stroking her warm golden fur, finally succeeded in taking my mind away from Sedge.

One day Stephan joined me. 'Why don't you take one home?' he asked. The idea caught me by surprise: for all the time I had been spending with these dogs, feeling joy that could not be suppressed when I saw their eyes open for the first time, it had never occurred to me to try to adopt one. If I had thought about it for too long I might have said no, worried that the guilt of trying to replace Sedge so soon would creep up on me as I tried to bond with a new puppy. But in the moment it felt right to take with me some piece of the only happiness I had been able to find in the weeks since he had gone. The lodge owner gave his agreement and before long we were researching the requirements for bringing a dog back with us to the UK. I had first picked the runt of the litter, having looked at how big the father was. But he had gone missing, a presumed victim of the ever-present lizards. So we chose another, slightly larger but with similar markings, the dark patch around his nose then covering almost half of his golden-brown face. He came with us on the next leg of our trip, when we moved into a Buenos Aires rented apartment.

There he reminded me exactly what it means to be a puppy parent. He happily set about tearing to bits the well-appointed front garden, shredding all of the beautiful plants with his teeth, turfing the mud out of the pots and spreading it across seemingly every inch of stone paving. He was at least living up to his name, Pacu; this is a fish closely related to the piranha, with incisors to match. Soon we realised what we had signed up for: a dog I had chosen because he was one of the smallest in the litter, but who grew and grew until he was closer to Stephan's size than mine, loving every play-fight and retrieving every stick thrown.

Part of me dreaded the moment when we would bring him home and he would begin to occupy territory that had once been Sedge's. But although the idea of replacing my most beloved dog felt wrong, I also knew that an empty space by my side was so much worse. There could never be another Sedge – an animal who felt almost human in his gentle spirit, constant attentiveness and limitless warmth. But once we were home, Pacu soon assumed his place next to me on the riverbank, responding to the screech of the reel and keeping an unrelenting eye on the fish, just as Sedge always had. Back on the waters I knew best, with the familiarity of a dog's loyal presence alongside me, I could at last begin the process of healing.

It is early, but the sun hitting my right arm fills me with warmth. Last night we were out while the sky was pink and trout were bubbling to the surface to feed on the vigorous hatch. In the misty morning light, the same water appears piebald, little white bubbles popping over its dark-brown surface. There is something sacred about fishing like this: at the very beginning of the day, alone with my dog, all possibilities unspoiled.

The river is low, calm and glassy, revealing the many moss-sprouting boulders strewn over its course. Pacu sits on one of them, dipping his nose below the surface to fish out sticks, which he brandishes hopefully in my direction. Not now. Clouds have descended, casting my arm back into shadow but sparking hope that the river might yield a catch before the day has properly begun. This grey sky is the angler's delight, coaxing the fish out of the hiding places into which sunlight drives them. The current meanders from left to right and then left again, traversing the stones that provide ready resting spots for salmon and sea trout.

As I follow the overgrown footpath alongside the river, smelling the wild garlic, hearing nothing except the onward rush of the river and birds lodged on out-of-sight branches, it is hard to believe that Newcastle is little more than twenty miles away. Everywhere I look is a different shade of green. Every sound I hear is one of nature's own. And best of all, once I have finished fishing this beat from top to bottom, I will have arrived back home.

The River Tyne was one I had fished often and knew well before Stephan and I decided to move there, finding a home within sight of its banks. More precisely, this is the North Tyne, its water darker and rockier, almost a different entity altogether than its southern stretch, which begins at Hexham. In fact, it is almost a Scottish river, with its early miles hugging the border before beginning the journey south. Perhaps it is this connection that means it has felt like home from the moment we came here. After my parents' divorce, my mother moved north to Scotland in part because she loved the salmon fishing so much. Now I have done my own version of the same, leaving behind Yorkshire with its memories of a marriage faltering and failing and making my life's next start by the water, near the salmon.

It was the trout that first lulled me into the rhythms of fishing, at the lake with my mother and brother, feeling the adrenaline of my first bites on the fly. But it is the salmon that worked its way into my heart. To watch a salmon in your net is not just to marvel at its strength and beauty, but to recognise a communion between angler and fish: two living beings each with their own life's path, which fate and chance have brought together on that day.

No matter where I have been in the world, or what exotic species I have been fishing for, it is salmon to which I always long to return, the fish that will never give up its secrets. I know the joy of cracking the enigma that is the Atlantic salmon will never fade, and the meaning of this fish will never be lost on me; each catch instantly recalls all those before it. Every time I hook into a salmon I am eleven years old again, deciding to release my first one back into the water. I am twenty-one, reeling in the Spey bar of silver that seemed to point the way towards a new way of life. And I am thirty, on the Kola Reserve in Russia, stunned and thrilled by the run of the *osenka*, which has reminded me that, even with so much fishing now behind me, there are still entire worlds I have yet to encounter.

The salmon continue to take me to new places and open up new experiences. This year, almost a decade after I first hosted a fishing trip, I got my first opportunity to guide (rather than just host) abroad, on the East Ranga River in Iceland. Accustomed as I was to guiding clients on English rivers where seeing a salmon jump is an event, working in Iceland was almost sensory overload. The country is renowned for its salmon rivers, and the East Ranga is one of the fishiest. The group I was guiding caught fish after fish, some experiencing that moment for the first time.

More special still was a coda to that trip that took me to the opposite end of the country, hundreds of miles north to the Big Laxa River. I had been contacted by a lodge with a story that intrigued me: the majority of their trainee guides on one of Iceland's foremost salmon rivers were women. And they were all from the same family; it was a tradition that had been passed down from one generation to the next, including to the owner's teenage children. I was contacted by Alli, who was making a film about the women anglers. He asked, would I like to be a part of it? No second invitation was needed, and on arrival at the airport I was met by Arni, the lodge owner, and his 14-year-old daughter, Áslaug. The following day she would be guiding me.

When we got into the boat the next morning, I

wondered if I should offer to row. But soon this tiny-looking girl had propelled us two hundred metres across the river and to the end of the beat, short of an adjacent waterfall. I took in our surroundings, somehow both desolate and welcoming, the bank sloping up gently on one side, the water feeling wide and hopeful as we waded into it. Then Áslaug was instructing me, in a clear, confident voice, to put my fly just above the falls, into the slower water where tired salmon would be resting after their ascent. I cast several times, watching the fly sweep round, almost taking for granted after a week of plentiful fishing that a bite would come. But none did, and I could sense my young guide's disappointment. This was her first time out guiding alone, trying to help someone land a salmon, and I was desperate not to let her down.

No amount of coaxing and casting would yield a response. The magnificent river, known for its vigorous grilse and salmon that have grown huge over multi-winter stays in the ocean, was passive. In the end we started wading back to the boat, smiling despite the fruitless venture. I was carrying my rod over my shoulder, as I always do, letting the line and fly trail through the water behind me, just in case. I have never been so shocked to feel a bite, with none of the usual rhythm and structure of the cast. But the salmon was right there below us, the hook set easily, and Áslaug needed no encouragement to move in with the net. Recognising something of myself in her careful determination was a poignant moment.

Women have always been a part of fishing's story, but the future of the sport should and will be more female than ever.

Female anglers are already to the fore in the United States, where women are much more prevalent as guides. Through the outdoors brand YETI, who I work with as an ambassador, I have met amazing women who are at the very top of their game, fishing for everything from trout and salmon to steelhead, bass and permit. And I have had the chance to fish in the US myself, for the first time since digging for clams on a childhood holiday to Maine. The destination was Venice, Louisiana, and the target was redfish – a huge marshland creature only found in North America, with the shape of a sea bass and the power of a wild carp. When they dip their heads to feed, their tails poke out above the water, revealing the distinctive black spot that is supposed to resemble an eye and fool predators into believing a tail is in fact a head.

In Venice, you are at the southernmost point of the Mississippi River accessible by road, at the very bottom of the Great River Road, which begins 3,000 miles to the north in Minnesota. The town styles itself as the Gateway to the Gulf (of Mexico). Locals and travel guides sometimes call it the end of the world. Beyond are only ports, coves, oil rigs and 530 miles of water until you hit Isla Holbox, where I had fished for tarpon on honeymoon. Out on the river boat, bringing in two magnificent redfish, I was reminded that I will never reach the point where I have seen everything that the rivers and oceans of the world have to offer – not even a fraction of it.

Trips like my Venice voyage excite me, but at the end of a long week, feeling the ache in your shoulders of long days on the water, living every moment of catches made and lost, it is home that I long to return to. Now more so than ever, in Northumberland, with the Tyne so close by. When the river app tells me that the water level has just started to lift, or it's dropping to the perfect height, the skies have clouded over and the day will be mild, I can be by the water in minutes, taking advantage of conditions that may be here one hour and gone the next; when the balance between angler and salmon is tilted just a little in favour of the pursuer. I check the weather and assess the conditions even when I know I will not be able to go fishing that day. Being so close to the water, and to the salmon, gives me a tingle when I wake up each morning during the season. Just the thought that I might catch a salmon that day is enough.

I had always wondered what it would be like to live near a great salmon river. Now I know. It was not always so for the Tyne: for over a century after the Industrial Revolution, the surrounding factories, refineries, mines and mills sucked oxygen out of the water and dumped chemicals in; cyanide, arsenic, lead and mercury among them. Water was drawn out and pumped back hot from the work of heavy industry. The river became a hostile environment for all living things and in the late 1950s was declared 'biologically dead'. Now tens of thousands of salmon return to its waters each year. The presence of a salmon hatchery, and extensive work to improve the quality of the water, have restored the Tyne to its historic status as a thriving home for migratory fish. Rivers, like people, are resilient when given the chance.

Moving here was not a decision made lightly, but I knew the time had come to leave Yorkshire. I stayed following the divorce because I could not abandon the fishing school while it still felt like a fragile newborn. But now, into our fifth season, with an established group of guides and a dedicated manager in place, and hundreds of people coming to learn to fish each year, it no longer needed me so close by. The work to build and develop the school is never done; each year brings a new set of challenges and some additional requirement for investment that reminds me this is not an industry to make your fortune in. But I no longer feel that, if I turn my back for a second, it might somehow cease to exist.

With distance has come perspective. For years I effectively lived above the shop, addicted to my work because working harder felt like the only way to guarantee survival. Behind every picture of a student making their first catch was a less photogenic reality of graft, compromise and even sacrifice. The school was the product of endless late nights and long days of worry about whether it would ever get off the ground; then, once it had, whether it would grow and become sustainable. Emails, planning spreadsheets and budgets became as much a part of my life as rods, reels and flies. When you are not making money, as in the early days, every line of expenditure makes you feel queasy, even though you know it is a necessary investment in the future you are trying to build.

Getting away has helped me to loosen those self-imposed shackles. There is more separation between work and the rest of my life, more time to pursue new interests like tying my own fishing flies. More opportunities for those precious early mornings where there is nothing else to think about except the water and the fish, the fly I will use and the flow of my cast. Just the chance to fish for fishing's sake: no client to guide, no concern for what I will post on social media.

I am also learning to appreciate and enjoy the water in different ways. Now when I return to the Test to guide, I also enjoy its unique waters a different way: by putting on a wetsuit so I can actually swim through the chalk stream, exploring the places where the fish cluster and hide, experiencing the river as they do, seeing what cannot be seen from above, even in water as clear as this. And when I am still standing on the bank, I look at water differently: with more patience and discernment, perhaps a little less eager than I once was but no less fascinated by what lies beneath. It's a picture I have taught myself to paint in more vivid details, assessing a stretch of river and being able to see immediately where it is running fast, the glassy pockets that hint at a deeper section, and the seams between two sections of current where a trout may be lying up. No river is uniform, and learning to appreciate the different depths, speeds, directions and colours on every stretch of water is all part of fishing's endless fascination.

More and more I now practise these skills on the Tyne, which has become my home river, the latest tributary in a fishing life encompassing some places I will never fish again and others to which I cannot stop myself from returning. Then come summer I head for the Spey, hiring a house and bringing friends for an annual Scottish holiday much as my parents used to do. Friends I have known for ever and others I have made through fishing all come together. As all our lives evolve and branch off on new paths, fishing remains a constant. Claire S., who I first met when she approached me at a fishing fair out of the blue, now has a son to whom I am godmother. So when we go out on the water, there are now small, wellingtoned feet dashing up and down the riverbank, taking me back to the days when I was too restless to hold a fishing rod for long but loved nothing more than to be by the water.

Like the salmon leaping over waterfalls to reach its natal river, I am unerringly drawn back to familiar waters like the Spey, back to where I first discovered what fishing really was, to where I first felt the surges of joy and pangs of frustration that accompany it, beginning to learn the skills that would set the course of my life. Something about the majesty and eternity of this river, one that is of course constantly changing but also feels reassuringly familiar, has made it the indispensable companion of my fishing life.

It is only as my life has progressed and undergone inevitable ups and downs that I have begun to fully appreciate the role that fishing plays in it. I have always known, almost since the day I found my way back to it in my early twenties, that it was a source of calm, a peacefulness that simply does not exist for me unless I am on and preferably in the water. But I have only gradually discovered that fishing is also a source of one of the most important facets of any life: of continuity and legacy. Fishing charts a course through my life as surely as the Spey carves a path through the Scottish countryside. There are wider sections where it dominates and narrower ones where it has dwindled almost into insignificance; some areas that catch the full glare of the sun and others that are consigned to shade. There are magnificent areas of forest and other patches that seem almost bare and featureless. If I think about where I was at any given point in my fishing journey, I can also tell you where I was on my life's journey – how I felt, the thoughts and concerns that were dominating my mind, the hopes and fears that I held. The places I have fished, the people I have fished alongside and the fish I have netted all mark points on the map of my soul.

Like Ariadne's thread, this unspooling line of fishing memories and experiences has led me out of some corners that felt dark and unnavigable. It connects many of the most important times in my life and also stretches into places outside my consciousness, into a past of stories I have read and been told – by my mother about her fishing experiences, about the women who paved the way for female anglers – and towards a future for which I can only have hopes and expectations. I have been able to tell myself that, as long as I hold on to the line, I will never truly be lost in life. I cling to it because I know, as no one can know at twenty-one, about the transience of life – how vows that were meant to be for ever can be unmade, how friendships that seemed eternal can become lost, and what it means to lose those closest to you.

Against this backdrop, the one thing on which I can truly rely, which is not subject to the vicissitudes of life or the vagaries of human relationships, is fishing. I know that, wherever I go and whomever with, my rod, reel and line will always be the most trusted of companions. I know that fishing will always be there for me, as eternal as the landscape it is a part of.

Now, there are no questions when a last-minute invitation arrives to go fishing somewhere exciting on the other side of the world. Like a trip back to the Seychelles, where I lost my head when I saw a shark pursuing the bonefish I had just caught and released, and had to be stopped from running after it to protect the fish. Stephan and I share in each other's adventures, as well as retaining the freedom to pursue our own. 'See you in the next place,' Stephan will say to me as one of us drops the other off at an airport.

I also know that, wherever in the world I may be going next, I will always be home again come the next domestic fishing season – to guide on the Test's gin-clear waters, to welcome both new and returning pupils to Swinton, and to revisit my greatest love of salmon fishing in Scotland.

Sometimes I have worried that I boomerang too much, seeking the stability of an idealised family life in one moment, and the freedom of travel in the next. But I've realised that this choice is a false one. Home doesn't have to mean one place, family doesn't have to entail being firmly rooted, nor does travel demand that you be rootless. I can chase the rivers and fish I've always dreamed of, while at the same time knowing that I can always return to the waters I know best. I accept that the comforts of home are not going to become a net I cannot escape; nor will the distance of travel take me too far away from what matters most.

As in so many parts of my life, this is a lesson fishing has taught me – that I can be all the versions of myself, in all the places I long to be. It has shown me how there is value in the familiar as much as there is excitement in the unknown; that there is beauty not just in learning something new but in practising the same skill over and over until it becomes a part of you, an instinctive physical language whose mechanics are woven into a part of the brain beyond conscious thought.

The glory of fishing is that it constantly reminds you of the need both to recall old lessons and to seek out new challenges. You are rewarded for the endless hours that it requires to grasp and then hone the fundamentals of technique, but also taxed with learning the endless nuances and variations that casting demands in different conditions and environments. You must continually try to improve your basic technique at the same time as embellishing it with new sophistications; like coming every year to repaint a house, only to find that each time a new storey has been added. When the legendary angler and casting instructor Joan Wulff was asked by a journalist how long it would take to become a 'truly great caster', her response said it all: 'It depends on how much mental anguish you want to sign up for. It took me fifty years to get to this point.'

As she suggested, it is both the beauty and the curse of fishing that it is destined to be unfinished work for anyone who commits themselves to the task. It is both daunting and tantalising to think that, for as long as I fish, that will remain the case. The journey will continue, but no finish line will ever be reached. There will always be another fly, another fish, another river.

'Come on, let's have one last go.'

The rich late afternoon light signalled that the end of the trip was approaching, after not just one blank day for our group but three. Like every UK river that summer, the Beauly was sitting low, starved of rain and short on fish. It had hardly seemed to matter. I was with some of the most important people in my life, doing what I loved: fishing for Scottish salmon with my brother Marcus, his friend Tom, whom I had fished with on the River Tyne a decade earlier, and my friend Holly, now Tom's new wife.

The final member of the party was my godfather, Adrian, who had been with me on the day I fought and lost the sea trout aged eight on the Spey. As he pointed out, this was the first time we had fished together since then, and it was he who suggested that the two of us go out again, just in case we could locate the elusive bite. Tom pointed us through the trees to a pool we had not yet touched, and we waded together through a small stream to its head. The evening was warm and the sun steady. I went first, tying on a sunray fly, an easy way to see if I could get any fish to rise. Soon I was into the rhythm of the Spey cast, moving quickly down the pool.

'You're a caster!'

I basked for just a second in the compliment before the other shoe fell. 'But I catch fish. And I'm going to get one you missed.' Adrian had started, working much more slowly and deliberately with me. I knew he had hooked into something when I heard him laughing, and I abandoned my own work to go and watch him bring in a beautiful grilse, just like my own very first sea trout had been. More amusement followed when we returned to the group and I had to admit that he had got the better of me – 'wiping my eye', in fishing speak. I grilled him on what exactly he had done to get the bite, and as we parted he presented me with his fly: a deceptively simple pattern, red wing with a bit of silver on a small brass tube. Even after all this time, the fishing equipment and experience was still being passed down.

The fishing had been forgettable – just one bite in three days between five of us – but the trip itself could not have been more meaningful. When my mother joined us one day for lunch it felt like all the people and parts of my fishing life together on one riverbank. I could close my eyes and be transported back to the lake in Donnington with Marcus, dragging our shrimp nets through the water, Mum warning us not to make too much noise. To the Spey aged eight, feeling the uncontrollable excitement of the snap of my line and the tug for which I was so unprepared. To the Oykel, where I had brought in my first ever salmon, wondering why they all said it was so difficult.

Much as fishing can immerse you in the moment, it also has a knack of causing ripples in the memory. After all the places I have been and all the talented anglers I have witnessed, when I think of fishing my first thought is still of my mother, in her tweeds, rolling off one neat cast after another. I see her fishing as I rushed down the bank, using a plastic bottle cut in half to scoop up the little salmon fry. I think of those summer days that get longer in the recollection and of the fish we caught, the most distant in time yet also the most vividly recalled. I think of all these pasts and look forward, too, to the day when I hope to have a family and children of my own. I know that one of the most precious things I will do as a mother is to put a net and rod in their hands and teach them as mine taught me.

Through fishing I can see all the lives I have lived and all those I hope now remain ahead of me. I know that I will never tire of its gentle rhythms and rigorous requirements, the familiar patterns of the river I know and the undiscovered depths of one I do not. Even the most dedicated angling tourist would probably admit that there is nothing quite like the river you know innately, as if some part of you had broken off and buried itself into the bank.

Most of all, I will never lose the thrill of what it is to catch a fish: one that never fades but carries different meanings as you go through life. In childhood the thrill was pure adrenaline, excitement and surprise. Into my twenties it became a mark of achievement, a way to measure progress and to feel purpose. And increasingly it is about the recognition of how small and fleeting these moments are, and how great the world surrounding them – the voyages of two lives colliding when a fish bites the fly and the line bulges with tension.

The struggle that ensues pits skill and technique against sheer will and survival instinct. Soon the tussle ends, but the journey does not. For most anglers, releasing the fish, returning it to the water and helping to restart its journey is as intrinsic to the process as casting and catching. It is a matter not just of sustainability and legality, but of morality and dignity. The fish, restored by its moment of rest, is ready to return and resume its journey. The chance set of circumstances that brought it onto the angler's line and into its net dwindles into memory. The river runs on, the fish swims out, and nature resumes its course.

Acknowledgments

In my wildest dreams, I never imagined that I would write a book about my life and my deepest passion, fishing. The serendipitous knock on my door from Tris Payne, Director of Broadcast for PFD, led to the realisation that my story was worth sharing. I am incredibly grateful for the encouragement and support I have had from Tris and Adam Gauntlett from PDF. I had a pinch me moment when Tris told me that we had offers from publishers not only the UK, but also the USA, Germany and Taiwan. Thank you to my editor Kirty Topiwala and the team at Hodder, and Kara Watson and the team at Simon and Schuster for being with me every step of the way.

I am an ordinary fisherwoman who has made fishing her life, and I just happened to be in the right place at the right time. I hope that my book will inspire those who have never held a fly rod to give it a try, for I believe it can be an immensely fun, therapeutic and rewarding experience.

This book has been written with the support and love of my partner in life and fishing, Stephan, my parents, stepmother, grandparents, brother, extended family and friends. A special thank you to Claire Sadler and Clare Brownlow for being there through thick and thin. To my dearest grandparents, thank you for always being there for me, for looking after me so well when I come to stay, and for providing me with non-judgmental advice whenever I've needed it.

With thanks to my casting mentors, especially Chris Hague and Sekhar Bahadur. I also want to express my appreciation for the exceptional team at the Northern Fishing School. Their support over the past five years have been instrumental in the growth and success of the business. I am incredibly fortunate to be surrounded by such a talented and dedicated group of individuals. I extend my gratitude to Richard from Tarn Graphics, whose exceptional graphic design skills have played a pivotal role in shaping the visual identity of my brands.

I have written this book in loving memory of Sedge, Uncle Timothy and Mick May. Uncle Timothy, my father's brother, was an extraordinary man. Despite a lifelong battle with kidney disease, a later diagnosis of Parkinson's, and ultimately succumbing to cancer, he exemplified resilience and positivity. Not once did I hear him complain; he consistently radiated joy upon seeing others and inquired about their news. Whenever I find myself facing a dreary day or indulging in complaints, I reflect on his optimism and strive to be a better person in those moments.

I extend my gratitude to Mick May for his graciousness during our phone conversation, where I enthusiastically shared my thoughts on his book and how it served as a profound inspiration for me. This inspiration catalysed the conception of an idea to offer complimentary fishing experiences to individuals affected by cancer and their companions. I am thrilled that we have already successfully established two venues in the UK, and we are on track to inaugurate our third. Mick's book not only sparked the idea but has become the driving force behind our mission to bring solace and joy to those facing the challenges of cancer.

Along the River Tyne, a plaque commemorates Sedge; a thoughtful tribute given to me by Stephan. 'A little dog wandered these river banks, by the name of Sedge "The Ledge". From 2015 - 2021 he brought joy to every angler from near and far. He loved roaming the countryside in all its splendour, just like you and me. We miss our companion and loyal friend.'

This book has been a constant companion throughout my life's ups and downs, offering comfort in times of both hardship and joy. Through the twists and turns of my experiences, writing has been a therapeutic outlet, allowing me to explore my emotions and make sense of my life. When facing personal struggles, it has been a safe space where I could lay bare my innermost thoughts and feelings, finding solace in the act of self-disclosure.

I first picked up a rod when I was 5 years old in 1995. Fishing took over my life 16 years later, and I have been passionate about it ever since. I hope to continue to share my love of the outdoors with others for many years to come.

Glossary

Beat: A stretch of river designated for fishing, up to a few miles long.

Blank day: A day when no fish are caught (which may still be a very enjoyable one).

Cast: The backward and forward motion of the fishing rod and line, used to propel the lure (fly) onto a target area of water. A technique with endless variations depending on the fish, water and conditions.

Catch and release: The practice of releasing fish back into the water after they have been caught. Extremely common in modern fishing when it comes to wild fish and especially endangered species such as Atlantic salmon.

Fly: The lure tied to the end of the fishing line, concealing the hook. Uses artificial materials to replicate the appearance of the aquatic creatures on which the fish feed. Main varieties include dry fly (used on the surface of the water), nymph (used under the surface) and streamers (pulled through the water to resemble swimming prey).

Fly fishing: Fishing technique based around use of the artificial fly, meticulously designed to mimic the insects, baitfish, or other prey that fish consume. In contrast to spin fishing, which uses weighted lures designed to rotate underwater and attract the attention of the fish (and which is most suitable when needing to cover larger stretches of water). In fly fishing the fly is extremely light and the line is weighted.

Ghillie: A traditional Scottish fishing guide and riverkeeper.

Grilse: An Atlantic salmon that has returned to its home river from the ocean after a single winter (most remain at sea for two or three years, enabling them to grow larger and increase their reproductive potential – if they can survive the perils of the ocean).

Guide: A fishing professional and often local expert, hired by visitors to help them fish a lake, river or stretch of ocean. A guide knows where and when fish gather, what kind of fly is most successful, and what cast you should use.

Haul: Tugging on the line during the backward and forward sections of the cast, to increase line speed and therefore distance.

Hook: The moment the fish has bitten on the fly and attached itself to the metal hook, giving the angler traction ('hooking in' to the fish). The word derives from Old English *angol*, hence 'angling' and 'angler' as synonyms for fishing and fisherman.

Host: The group leader and/or tour organiser on a fishing trip, making arrangements and ensuring people are looked after. Distinct from the guide, who is focused purely on fishing.

Knot: Technique used to tie together fishing lines and lures. Typical varieties include a half-blood knot, used to attach a fly: the line is passed through the eye of the hook, wrapped multiple times back round itself, and fed back through the loop before being pulled tight. A blood, or clinch, knot uses a similar technique to tie two pieces of line together, with each knotted round the other. A perfection loop serves multiple purposes, such as securing a fly at the end of a line or joining two lines together with a loop-to-loop connection.

Matching the hatch: In fly fishing, the task of trying to replicate the feeding habits of a fish by choosing a fly that most closely resembles its intended next meal. A subject of constant debate in fishing shops and on riverbanks. 'Hatch' refers to the point at which flies emerge from or near the water in their winged form, bringing more fish to the surface, which means prime time for anglers.

Mend: Manipulating the fly line to prevent the fly from moving too slowly or being dragged too quickly by the current.

Migratory fish: Fish such as salmon and sea trout that are born in rivers, migrate to the ocean to feed and mature, and then return to the river to spawn.

Natural presentation: In fly fishing, presenting the fly in such a way that most closely matches how the creature itself would be moving on or through the water.

Playing the fish: Work done by the angler between hooking into a fish and completing the catch. A fish will often seek to 'run', to unhook itself and escape its pursuer. Playing the fish means giving the fish enough line to tire itself out over one or several runs, before picking the right moment to apply pressure and bring it in to be netted. Applying force too soon can lead to a tug-of-war that will snap the line or dislodge the fly. Using insufficient force, which leads to a slack line between the rod tip and the fly, can easily cause the fly to dislodge from the fish's mouth.

Pool: A deeper, slower-moving, often sheltered section of river where fish are liable to gather to rest, attracting the interest of anglers. A 'pool' also refers to a specific segment of the 'beat'. For instance, on the Nutwith beat at the Swinton Estate, the top two renowned salmon pools are identified as 'Madges' and 'Roman Ford'.

Reel: Mechanical device attached to the rod, used to store spooled fishing line and apply drag to control resistance when a fish is running.

Set: The movement made to secure the hook after the fish has taken the fly. Depending on the fish, this can involve tugging on the line (strip set), sharply lifting the rod upwards (lift set), or a combination of the two (strip strike), and in the case of a salmon it is simply a pause, wait for the fish to turn and lift.

Stocked fish: Fish that have been artificially bred before being released into a waterway, allowing fisheries to maintain the population.

Strip: The process of manually pulling on the line after casting, whether to keep the line tight, facilitate movement of the fly through/over the water, or in some cases set a hook.

Take: The moment when a fish bites the fly and the angler can feel resistance on the line.